A Cat Named Petunia

Tales of 23 Cats & the People Who Loved Them

A Cat Named Fatima

Tales of 23 Cats & the People Who Loved Them

James Kenyon DVM

From T. S. Eliot to Andrew Lloyd Webber — cats and their personalities are told. These true stories are but a few of those characters and their owners who have enriched my life.

Happy Trails
James Kenyon

the Barn Swallow
OKOBOJI IOWA
OPEN 7 DAYS A WEEK ALL YEAR

Meadowlark PRESS
Emporia, Kansas, USA

Meadowlark Press, LLC
meadowlark-books.com
meadowlark-books.square.site
PO Box 333, Emporia, Kansas 66801

A Cat Named Fatima:
Tales of 23 Cats & The People Who Loved Them
www.jamesrkenyon.com

Cover art by Barbara Steward Kenyon:
Painting is of the actual Fatima and the author's daughter, Jennifer, 1980.

Interior art by Thomas Marple

Meows Font by Aisyah (commercially licensed)
https://www.creativefabrica.com/designer/nuraisyahamalia1729/ref/369973

The essays in this book are works of creative nonfiction; accounts of events as told to the author by the parties. Conversations and details are inspired by the subject's stories and filled in by the author's imagination.

PETS / Cats / General
PETS / Essays & Narratives
BIOGRAPHY & AUTOBIOGRAPHY / Personal Memoirs

ISBN: 978-1-956578-05-8 (paperback)
ISBN: 978-1-956578-06-5 (hardback)

Library of Congress Control Number: 2021951940

To the myriad of cats I have treated in my forty years in veterinary practice.

Also by James Kenyon

The Art of Listening to the Heart

A Cow for College and Other Stories of 1950s Farm Life

Golden Rule Days: History and Recollections of 109 Closed Kansas High Schools

Echoes in the Hallway: History and Recollections of 102 Closed Iowa High Schools

Cat Tales

Confession

I have loved cats since I was old enough to hold them. As a towheaded five-year-old, I have memories of carrying "my" first litter of kittens to the house in a cardboard box for my mother to see. I recall the cats on the farm I grew up on, standing on their back legs to catch the streams of milk I squirted into their mouths as I hand-milked our Brown Swiss cows in the old limestone barn.

When a client would ask, "Doc, what is your favorite animal?" I never went public with my answer. I didn't want to offend the dog owners, the horse owners, the exotic animal owners. But now, I say, "The cat is out of the bag. Cats are and always have been my favorite species."

This book honors a few of the cats I have met over the years and their adoring and faithful human companions.

James Kenyon, DVM

Barn Cat

Ode to Barn Cat

Dear little Barn Cat had only three legs,
Went through life without even a peg.
Had a bobbed tail, the tip was white.
Came running when her girl was in sight.

From a nice family, but an allergy for the wife,
Destined to the barn for the rest of her life.
Lived there first with Skip the horse,
Then came Paul's pigs, to her remorse.

She rode on the shoulder of the girl in the saddle.
Perched there round her neck with legs astraddle.
Saddend when the girl went to college at Dordt.
Soon a Dutchman came home to court.

Moved to apartment with these newlyweds.
Indoors at last and very well fed.
Slept in the greyhound's bed, made him sleep on the floor,
Lived nine lives and a few more.

arn Cat—what a name! It has been given to scores of Felidae for millennia, bringing images of a wily, tough mouser who is master of the pride. Barn Cat's story begins with a little girl, Renee, riding her horse, Skip. The pair departed early one morning for a daily ride in the woods and a trail by the Shell Rock River. A kitten was crouched along the gravel path. Renee spotted the small black and white feature in the short buffalo grass. Renee was thirteen years old with long, brunette braids and a freckled face that accented her complexion. She dismounted her horse and knelt to touch and cradle the pitiful little meowing furball.

"Oh, you poor little one. How did you ever get out here all by yourself?" she whispered.

She picked the crusts away from around the kitten's eyes and wiped the little stuffy nose on her shirtsleeve. The kitten's tearing eyes and thin bony ribs were clues of abandonment on this isolated country river road. After a moment of cuddling, Renee tucked the kitten down the front of her red flannel shirt. Skip's nostrils flared and his eyes opened wide, indicating his apprehension about this stranger. Renee slowly climbed back into the saddle using one hand to protect the wiggling kitten under her shirt. It clung with its tiny sharp claws digging into her chest.

Skip pranced back up the ravine and through the grader ditches to get back home. Holly Crandall, Renee's mother, was weeding in the rose garden at the country ranch home and immediately noticed her daughter's hand clutching the front of her shirt over the heart area. She met them near the circular driveway and was amazed to see movement beneath Renee's red flannel shirt.

"Mom, you're not going to believe this! I found this pitiful little kitten down along the river road path. Someone must have dumped her off because there were no signs of any other cats in the brush," blurted Renee, out of breath with excitement.

The family had never been able to have an indoor animal, as one of Renee's younger brothers and her mother Holly were allergic to cat dander. With the loving care of a nurse, Holly accepted this rescue kitty. It would have to stay in the garage or in the horse barn, and so the name was an instant agreement between Renee and her family. Barn Cat became Renee's constant companion.

The trip to the veterinarian the next day was memorable. Little Barn Cat seemed to have every parasite known to cathood. From ears to tail, she was de-mited, dewormed, defleaed, and deloused. In time, her eyes stopped watering and this little ugly duckling's hair coat began to shine. The potbelly, protruding ribs, and the gooey sniffles all disappeared.

Though Barn Cat was relegated to the barn, she seemed to prefer the stable. Its smells and soft straw bales in the manger provided good spots for sleeping. The kitten looked forward to dawn when the little girl calling, "Barn Cat!" from the back deck of the house appeared, promising food. Barn Cat came running like a dog chasing a rabbit. In two leaps she was up the steps and onto the legs of Renee's blue jeans, which the kitten used as a ladder to get into the girl's arms. This summer routine of breakfast call, riding on Skip, and endless hours with the little girl became routine. When Skip was saddled and mounted, Renee patted her leg and the jeans-climbing cat would skedaddle up and onto the girl's shoulders. The cat planted herself in place with no seat belt, no helmet, and no fear of Skip walking, trotting, or even racing to get home from the trails.

Barn Cat was also a frequent visitor to the surrounding neighborhood houses. Posh little ranch style homes with acreages for horses made life at Buck Ridge a quiet country community. The neighbors were often honored to receive a gift from Barn Cat in the form of a dead rabbit, chipmunk, or frog on their back steps for them to admire. A recipient knew that Barn Cat had been on the prowl the night before. Her nocturnal hunting skills were the envy of every owl living in an oak tree along the river.

What a first summer it was for Renee and the luckiest cat on the ridge. The girl talked with her cat like an adult to a child and explained that she would be leaving for school in late August. Renee told Barn Cat about the yellow bus, books, carrying a lunchbox every day, and even the dress clothes that would replace her dusty and comfortable riding jeans. Barn Cat would tilt her head with every word, her eyes intently watching the girl. Sometimes Renee thought she saw Barn Cat's nod that she understood.

The day came when, in the distance, a loud engine was heard stopping and going, stopping and going, and the noise came closer and closer to Barn Cat's hideaway. She ran to the house to see what was happening and witnessed her little girl in braids, carrying a lunchbox. Renee walked out the front door, down the steps, and got on the big yellow school bus. As Renee boarded, she turned to wave to her mother and blew a kiss to Barn Cat who sat watching from the driveway.

4

A long, lonely day got better when Barn Cat heard again the singing of that motor coming down the road. She sat on the front steps and watched as the big yellow bus stopped in front of the house. The door folded outward, and the girl appeared. She patted her leg and called, "Barn Cat!" The black and white blur raced to the girl who was kneeling to greet her.

"You wonderful little kitty," Renee said. Barn Cat was in her arms in one leap. "I told you I would return. I could see you from the window on the school bus, and you waited here for me," Renee whispered. Her two brothers came off the bus, skipping and yelling at each other.

"Let me change out of these clothes," Renee said. "Let's head to the barn!"

For the next year, this routine was repeated. The bus would take Renee away and Barn Cat would wait on the front steps; the bus would return and off the pair would go for a horse ride. The girl, the cat, and the horse were inseparable on weekends. All the neighbors enjoyed seeing the girl on the big sorrel horse with Barn Cat riding on her shoulder. Horses from the numerous paddocks greeted them and kicked up their heels when they passed. Dogs in the yards just stared at this unusual cat, which seemed off limits for them to chase.

The following summer, Barn Cat's life was changed forever when she went on a predawn hunt for fieldmice. The dew glistened and the July morning was still. Knee-high alfalfa was in full bloom, ready to harvest, and lavender blossoms were at their peak. The fragrance permeated the air. The haze of early morning was starting to lift.

The noise of a tractor could be heard close by. Barn Cat hid low to the ground in the alfalfa. A strange, chattering sound reverberated as she hunkered pensively, listening, and waiting as the chattering came closer. She was frightened by the loud noise, the slithering movement approaching, and became alarmed as the cutting bar came slashing through the forage. Barn Cat managed to leap and miss most of the lethal sawing action of the cutter as the alfalfa in its path was flattened, but she screamed in pain and dragged herself to the tall thick bluestem at the edge of the field along the fencerow. Using only her front legs, she crawled.

Reaching the protected shade, Barn Cat collapsed and started to nervously pant. She could see that her leg had been severed above the knee. A jagged, porcelain-shiny bone protruded, and blood matted her fur and white tummy.

She whimpered and was frightened by her plight.

No one knew where she was or how severely injured. The green bottleflies soon swarmed like buzzards to their prey. Only now did she notice that part of her tail was also gone.

After a brief rest, Barn Cat used all her strength and dragged herself under the wooden fence into a nearby, dry and powdery dirt paddock. Seeking shelter, she pulled herself toward a nearby horse stable. She had been known to use it as a nighttime shelter in times of rain and bad weather while out on a hunt. Now it was to be her refuge.

The barn flies were still buzzing her, and the gnats were attracted to the drying blood on her fur. She did not try to use her other back leg, just pulled herself toward the barn until she reached the cool shade of the doorway.

Dusty, the pampered chestnut mare who lived in the stable, jumped in surprise. Barn Cat crawled with determination under the stable gate to the feed room, a place to hide. Using her last bit of energy, she sidled behind a gunnysack of oats. Her tail throbbed, but the severed leg felt numb. Barn Cat passed out and slept for a time.

She was awakened by the voice of a man. Dusty's whinny foretold that it was time for the morning feeding. The man, Fred, lived in the woods with his wife of many years. He fed Dusty religiously, twice daily, and at the same time each day.

Fred was saying things in horse-talk, like, "Oh you are so pretty this morning," and "Is our girl ready for her oats?" when he spotted the trail of blood and marks on the earthen floor. He moved the sheltering oat bag and found little Barn Cat. He hastily threw a square of timothy in the feed rack for Dusty and went running to the house for help.

Fred threw open the back door and yelled to his wife. "Betts, you have to call Holly. I think Barn Cat is in our stable dying."

The Crandall's phone number was on the notecard of frequently called numbers under a magnet on the front of the refrigerator.

The push-button phone rang.

"Holly, this is Betts. Can you come as soon as possible? Fred thinks Barn Cat is in our stable and may be dying."

When she hung up, Betty went into action. "Fred, you get a box. I'll bring a bathroom towel and meet you in the stable."

As they were leaving the house, they could already see Holly running across the field of freshly mowed alfalfa. She had taken the shortcut from her ranch house to reach the stable at the same time as the Hoffmans.

Fred warned, "Holly, this may not be Barn Cat, but it surely looks like her to me. Let's be quiet so as not to scare her. She may already be gone."

"I understand," Holly blurted, still out of breath from the dash across the field.

When the door was opened, they waited briefly for their eyes to adjust from the bright sunny morning to the darkness of the stable.

"Here's the kitty," Fred said as he bent down. He held a soft terrycloth bath towel in his hands. "Good, she's still here, and I don't see any new blood on the dirt. So, is this Barn Cat?"

"Yes. It's her alright. The poor little thing must be in terrible pain. We should take her to the vet and have her put to sleep," Holly gasped. "It looks like she is missing a leg and part of her tail."

Fred cupped Barn Cat in his hands and laid her on the towel in the brown cardboard box. She looked up at him and made no attempt to move. Her glazed eyes gave an approving look. She knew she was being helped.

The Cherokee jeep ambulance seemed to be crawling as the three of them—Fred, Betts, and Holly—made haste to the awaiting veterinarian. Pulling into the driveway, they were amazed to see a new veterinary graduate, Dr. Kathy, motioning where to park. Clad in her white uniform, she opened the back door of the Cherokee to find Holly holding the box and softly caressing Barn Cat's head.

Holly was emotional. "You won't believe this. She is purring! I don't think there is anything that can be done. She has lost a lot of blood and at least one of her legs has been severed off. What do you think?"

The doctor softly petted Barn Cat while assessing her condition. "Well, she has good color, and I do not see any fresh blood, so there is hope that we can save her. What's her name?"

All three answered at the same time, "Barn Cat."

"Well then, Barn Cat, let me carry you into the hospital and see how we can patch you up." Kathy used her most reassuring and soft mother voice and smiled. She gently slid her arms under the box and carried it through the emergency room door, leading the parade into the clinic.

With the examination light brightly shining on the patient, the young doctor carefully plucked the straw and grass off the bloody stump and fur. She rinsed the dirt away with soft saline and iodine scrub squares.

Seeing the extent of the damage, assessing the protruding jagged femur, Holly gasped. "Oh Doctor, surely there is no way she can live. Shouldn't we put her out of her misery?"

Dr. Kathy answered, "This stump can be freshened up and the muscle ends pulled over it, and there appears to be plenty of skin to cover the site."

"But how will she ever be able to have balance to walk without part of her tail," Holly said with a wince. "She's an outdoor cat and lives in our garage and barn at nights."

"You may not believe it, but she will be able to run and jump and do just fine with three legs, and the tail really doesn't have anything to do with balance," Dr. Kathy said kindly.

Fred and Betts, who had been nervously waiting in the reception area, could not stand it any longer. They cracked the door open to see what the verdict might be.

Fred asked, "Is there any chance she will make it?"

"Oh, I believe there is more than a chance," Dr. Kathy confidently reassured them. "Barn Cat may only have eight more lives to spare, but this could have been worse."

"Well then, please do what you can. My husband is a physician, and we have four children, so I guess we can bring her home to our garage if she lives." Holly smiled, knowing she had just committed to caring for a handicapped kitty. "Barn Cat, you will be loved whether you have all of your legs or not. Our little Renee loves you so much, and she will nurse you till you are back to full strength."

The veterinary technician prepared the surgery room. This black and white kitty had beautiful tuxedoed markings. Her underbelly was white, and the outside of her thigh on the severed leg had black fur. The front leg was shaved with a vibrating clipper, and a small catheter was placed in the cephalic vein. A slow drip of lactated Ringer's solution was started to help restore some of the lost fluid to Barn Cat's circulatory system. Anesthetic was added to the IV, and the cleanup and surgical preparation commenced.

The jagged, sawtooth end of the glistening white femur bone was freshened and cut at midshaft with a bone saw to leave a clean, transverse surface at the end of the remaining bone. With meticulous detail, the frayed muscles of the quadriceps were wrapped around the end of the stump and closed with small sutures. The remaining skin was neatly sutured over the muscle layer with the suture line matching the black and white fur over the incision.

Barn Cat remained on the IV for another hour and was moved to the recovery ward. Within two hours, she was sitting up and responding to the technician as if nothing had happened.

"Oh, you sweet little kitty," cooed Dr. Kathy as she peeked into the cage to check on her patient. The heating pad had kept Barn Cat warm, and she seemed irritated with the IV tubing

8

attached to her leg. With her recovery going so well, the tubing was removed, and she made her first attempt to the litter pan with only one back leg. No problem as she braced herself daintily over the pan like a gymnast doing a handstand.

It was midafternoon when Holly brought Renee to visit little Barn Cat at the hospital. She had prepared her daughter by telling her about the accident and let her know that her beloved kitty might never be able to walk on her own again. Expecting the worst, they were ushered into the cat ward where Barn Cat greeted them. She was rubbing the front of the cage door and meowing her message, *You will never believe what happened to me today.*

"Mother, she doesn't seem to act like anything even happened!" cried Renee.

"Well, look at you," Dr. Kathy remarked as she was going about her rounds. "I bet you are hungry, and it has been a long day." She opened a small tin of recovery formula and Barn Cat licked the bowl clean. She had been waiting hours to be served dinner.

Dr. Kathy told Renee, "Barn Cat came through the surgery with flying colors. I believe she should stay the night here to recover quietly and should be able to go home tomorrow morning."

Back home the next morning, Renee carried Barn Cat into the open garage. There was a new, clean plaid blanket in her platform bed. Not fearing anything, she jumped out of Renee's arms. Barn Cat seemed anxious to be home just twenty-four hours after her innocent hunting trip and tragic accident that nearly cost her life. She walked around the bed, assessing the new digs, and went back to Renee. The cat climbed up her jeans and curled around her neck, just as she always had. No one could ever detect that having only three legs changed anything in her routine.

"Okay, Barn Cat, we are home together again, but before we go riding, I have to practice the flute." Girl and cat climbed the steps to the deck, and Renee opened the rectangular, black felt case and assembled the three-piece silver shiny flute. Barn Cat had always hated the noise that came from the instrument. The whistling vibrations would send her jumping down, retreating to the garage as if to say, *You know, I really don't like that oblong silvery noise box. Just get it over with so we can go play.*

And play they did. Barn Cat loved riding horses. When in the barn together, Renee saddled up Skip, stepped into the stirrups, and patted her leg. Barn Cat came darting from the hay bales, crawled up Renee's jeans, jumped to her shoulder, and curled around her neck for a high vantage point horse ride.

For the next four years, Renee and her three-legged Barn Cat were inseparable. The handicap never slowed Barn Cat down from hunting and playing hide and seek with anyone caring to play the game. When found, she would leap high and bring joy to the game. She never learned to enjoy the flute and was even more offended when Renee became accomplished on the piccolo, too.

❅ ❅ ❅ ❅

All relationships change with age. Renee's long braids were gone. Activities at school altered some of the daily horseback riding routines. A second horse, Jolie Tashee Pone, joined Skip in the paddock. She was so named because Renee was taking French at the time, and it was a variation of "pretty spotted pony." Jolie was never part of Barn Cat's rides. When the day came for Renee to leave for college, Barn Cat's care was left to the family. She had never been much for using a litter pan, and the whole outside was her domain. With just a few kibbles in the food bowl, she was content to hunt for mice and other wild prey.

Her girl was off to college. Renee loved Barn Cat and had saved her from the gravel road and been her constant companion. Renee came home each holiday and school break. Barn Cat seemed to know just when her friend was to arrive. She would wait on the front steps, listening for the car as it crossed the nearby railroad tracks. Having meticulously cleaned her face and preened until her fur shone, she would run to the car with joy to see her friend and riding mate.

Even when a tall, blonde boyfriend arrived for Thanksgiving, Barn Cat was not offended. But she was happiest when it was just her and her dear friend alone. They talked in the barn about life and school and even boyfriends.

Following a summer wedding, Barn Cat was at last able to move in with Renee and a very understanding husband. They made regular trips to the country to see Skip and the wonders of nature and smell the fresh grass and alfalfa fields. They stopped to see the Hoffmans and returned to the scene of Barn Cat's accident to greet a nervous Dusty in her stable.

When a new dog was introduced to Renee's home, the question was, who would be in charge?

That's right. Barn Cat made up the rules. The greyhound, Spencer, was quickly put in his place and spent a lot of time whining and looking helpless while Barn Cat slept in his bed. Barn Cat lived a comfortable life in town with three children and two more dogs in the home. She never strayed from the house and seemed most content when making her last few trips to the country to sit on the shoulders of her girl as they rode a now graying, twenty-five-year-old Skip.

Beethoven

Ode to
Beethoven, the Alley Cat

Found under a dumpster, in a December snow.
Rescued by a skier, a cultured cat now.
This Vermont farm boy with a big heart.
Took him to class to a professor to part.

Three little girls at Christmas he came.
This alley cat needed a name.
Sat at the Steinway, the scales he was loving.
Chopin and Brahms, but Beethoven was chosen.

Tuna his favorite but liked anything fish.
Slept at night with any girl he wished.
The saltwater tank was a favorite draw.
Perched on the edge and dipped in his paw.

Taken to the vet for his little snip job.
Liked the place though his jewels were robbed.
Slipped out the door on a rainy night.
To the alley and warehouse, he meowed out of sight.

But for a hook in the mouth of a fisherman's dog,
'Twas rescued again, that night in the fog.
Now homebound for good, this musical cat,
Operas, classicals, and arias like that.

It was a cold, blustery December morning far away in middle America. A faint meowing was heard near the inner-city railroad tracks along a quiet, dead-end alley. A dusting of snow had painted the earth white, and the flakes coated the barren tree branches in glittering rime. This white-carpeted trail was punctuated with chickadee footprints, and a cross country skier with an agile frame ambled out for his morning gliding workout along the smooth trail along the Cedar River. The skier heard the noise as it penetrated the predawn stillness. From under the dumpster came a desperate *meow, meow, meow.* Already late for his workout, the skier bent down to peek under the rusty old dumpster and dug the snow away from the wheels. He spotted a wee little gray and white Jellicle kitten shivering and soaked beneath the snowy hideout. Hissing and yowling, the kitten backed further under the dumpster.

The man muttered, "Alright you little alley cat, be that way—so long, I can't help you anyway." Troy glided off.

On the horizon, billowing clouds of steam rose from the utilities power plant smokestack and drifted up against the low hanging gray clouds. Growing up in New England on his family's Vermont dairy farm, there was always an ample number of cats to love and feed. Each morning of his youth he witnessed the cats curled up and nestled next to the warm sides of the gold and white Guernsey cows laying on the straw bedding. The cats would rise and greet Troy's dad, squinting at the bright, incandescent lights and stretching with their front paws reaching out, their lumbar spines and tails raised. They knew the cows would soon be standing up in their stanchions. The cats scampered to the milk house for their breakfast of kibble and scraps from the kitchen. Having always loved every cat at home, Troy could not get the little alley kitten out of his mind as the crisp wind blew in his face. Frost formed on his eyelashes and moustache as he pushed himself along the trail.

He glided over Krieg's Crossing pedestrian bridge and looped around the five-mile trail in George Wyth Park. He concentrated and picked up his pace as he hurried back home. Leaving the trail, he was compelled again to kneel in the alley to look under the dumpster, noting the meowing had subsided. Yet, there was the little creature, curled up in a fetal position. This time, he reached to touch the kitten and there was no resistance. Taking off his warm, sweaty mittens, his large hands enveloped the skinny, damp kitten and carefully placed it in his coat pocket. Just two doors down the alley was his back stoop. He stepped out of his skis and boots and ascended the steps to the landing. The kitten had not moved beyond an occasional shiver and made no sound. In the small apartment kitchen, he slipped his coat off and gently lifted the pitifully small, cold creature out. Troy pondered. The kitten could not be more than a few months old. How could it have been left outside alone or found its way to the shelter of the dumpster?

"Okay, you little alley cat—it's you and me—and I have to be in class in a short time." Troy located a soft yellow terry towel and dried the kitten's fur as best he could. An empty plastic milk jug was filled with hot water and the towel was tented over it with the kitten securely hidden under the canopy.

As Troy stripped out of his ski pants, he muttered, "If I had known I was having a guest for breakfast, I would have done some shopping. All I have to offer you is some Half and Half from the fridge. I will be back in a couple of hours."

He poured a few tablespoons of the cold, thick cream into a plastic lid and popped it in the microwave to warm it to room temperature. Then he carefully positioned the lid under the towel tent. On his hands and knees, Troy picked up the still-shivering little body and dipped the kitten's nose in in the liquid. Blowing bubbles and sputtering, the kitten quickly came to life and ravenously lapped up the treat.

"Okay, little guy, you wait here, and I'll return soon with better cuisine for you."

As Troy left the apartment, he flipped on the radio to KUNI, broadcasting from WBUR Boston, his favorite station as a boy. He thought some sound would be more comforting for the kitten than dead silence.

He trekked to the music hall at the Gallagher Bluedorn Performing Arts Center across campus for a Music Theory class. The piano practice rooms were active as he entered the music wing. He met his piano instructor as he hurried down the hallway. Troy told her of his morning adventure, of finding the kitten under a dumpster. Dr. Burkholder, his stoic piano instructor, was recently divorced, and he knew that she had three little girls to support. As he shared his morning events, his teacher seemed to warm to his cat story.

"Well, that is quite a saga," she said, smiling as she backed away. "You know Troy, let me know how your little alley cat is doing or if you find a home for it. I may know someone who would be interested in adoption."

Troy smiled with relief and slid away to class where he was also assisting as a graduate student.

The snow had not subsided but had increased in intensity by the end of the hour-long class. Troy mused several times about the hissing kitten, trying to defend itself under the dumpster. The clock on the wall seemed to be in slow motion as the hour dragged on. With the last score completed, the professor said, "Looking outside, this may be a great day to get out a few minutes early. Go and enjoy this beautiful, fluffy snow."

That was great news to Troy. He grabbed his jacket and backpack. The stocking hat had not dried from his morning workout, and water beads glistened on the woolen edges. He considered stopping by the library to work on the paper for an impending deadline but decided it could wait for now. His own growling stomach reminded him that the kitten was also likely hungry.

Unfortunately, like most college campuses, there was no grocery store nearby. Troy had a friend in an apartment near campus who had cats. Maybe that would be the easiest place to beg for some food to take home to his alley cat. It was still mid-morning as he rapped on Monica's door. Still in her flannel pjs, she cracked the door to see a snow-covered Troy.

"Hey, can I step in a sec to ask a favor of you?" he pleaded. Monica was another grad student, and he had favored her for her Irish green eyes and porcelain complexion. Troy stomped off the wet snow from his boots and shook his jacket. He explained his predicament and the events of his crazy morning exercise in the woods.

"You softy," Monica said. "All I have is Puss 'N Boots, but here is a tin for my contribution." Her dimples stood out prominently as she looked up at him, admiring her friend's sensitivity.

Away down the steps, his boots crunching in the accumulating snow along the walks, Troy returned to his flat. Entering, his eyes were still trying to focus from the bright white landscape. He peered into the makeshift hot water bottle tent. Huddled next to the milk jug was Alley Cat. Troy could see a breathing motion as the gray and white fur methodically raised and fell with each respiration.

Troy popped the lid on the cat food, grabbed a tablespoon, and placed a spoonful in the can lid. He added an equal amount of Half and Half and made it into a slurry. Five seconds in the microwave and the tempting combination looked and smelled very appealing. "Okay little kit—see what you think of this," he mumbled as he awakened the skinny kitten. Alley Cat needed no prompting. He licked and gulped and growled, all at the same time.

Troy had not even taken off his coat as he knelt and enjoyed the scene. "Another life saved," he mused and smiled to himself. But now the gravity of rescuing this little rascal dawned on him. "I'm leaving in a week for Colorado to ski for a month with my buddy. Who can I get to take this poor little alley cat and give it a home and life?" he wondered.

He remembered Dr. Burkholder's concerned face.

For now, his job was to provide the kitten with food and warmth. He also knew that what goes in must also come out. Drawing on his boots again, he went out the door and down the steps to the alley with an empty coffee container. The snow continued its relentless accumulation. At the street, he found a barrel of sand placed strategically to be scattered by motorists in times of ice in intersections. Scooping the moist sand into the coffee can, he returned home. His early morning footprints were quickly covered, and he checked the dumpster under which AC had hidden. He could not see any daylight below it by this time. This storm was just getting a good start, and the sky was getting dark. Lights flickered as Troy rummaged through the trash can to locate a discarded pie tin. The sand was emptied into the tin and pushed under the warm tent for AC to hopefully use as a litter pan.

Troy refilled the water jug with hot tap water and called his rescue mission a success. He spread out his paperwork on the red and white vinyl tablecloth his mother had given him for the apartment and settled in to complete a tedious writing assignment, his final examination for Music Theory class.

Troy's ears were tuned into the scratching sound under the tent, and he knew that AC had used his instincts to find the makeshift sandy litter box to relieve himself. Then came the sound of a shuffling that seemed to last for minutes as the little creature tried to cover up the movement. "How can Mother Nature work her miracles and pass on that trait to even the mind of a baby kitten?" Troy pondered.

Over the course of the next day, feeding small tablespoon portions of the gruel, emptying the sandy litterbox, and reheating the water jug, Troy's quest to find a more permanent home for the kitten became a mission.

Following a night's sleep, an early morning skiing workout, and trek to class, Troy got his plan in place as he met Dr. Burkholder in the hallway of the music wing. "Mrs. Burk—I mean, Dr. Burkholder," he said.

"Please, just call me Linda."

"Well, yeah, I was just wondering if you, uh. Oh, I was just thinking if you . . . maybe you knew . . ." He stammered and fidgeted, looking for the right words.

"You mean to say, would I consider helping you out by taking that little homeless kitten to give to my girls for Christmas?" she asked.

"Wow, that's exactly . . . I mean, how did you know? I just can't care for it under my current circumstances." Troy said.

That night, Linda and her three little girls knocked at the backdoor of Troy's apartment. Alley Cat was playing with a ball of string when the girls removed their boots and started pulling the ball across the kitchen floor. They scooped him up, and each girl took a turn hugging and passing the cat on to the next sister. Alley Cat seemed to be smiling, or at least did not appear afraid as he meowed at the attention and dug his claws into their woolen jackets.

"Momma, this is the best Christmas present of all time," the oldest exclaimed.

Snuggled under a pea jacket, Alley Cat was out the door and off down the alley from where he was rescued.

The love he received from the trio of girls could have not been better scripted. Linda was firm in trying to confine Alley Cat to a carrier in the kitchen during the day when the girls were away at school. This rule lasted only a few days as the rambunctious scamp won everyone's heart. The Christmas tree was such a temptation, as more than once he gave it his best effort to climb the trunk to sit on the unsteady branches. Only after a free-falling bulb hit him as he ascended did he call off his adventures with the balsam.

Weeks turned into months, winter into spring, and this adorable gray and white fuzzball grew into a debonair youth. The name Alley Cat, or just AC, had been shortened even further to Alley. During the girls' piano lessons, Alley leaped onto the back of the baby grand and watched intently as the hammers lifted and fell on the strings. He tilted his head, rapt with attention, as each of the girls practiced for their mother. It is seldom that three siblings like to practice their piano lessons in one home. However, in the Burkholder home, it became a contest to see who could get to the piano first just to have Alley perform with his conducting. By family vote, Alley's name was officially changed to Beethoven after the maestro pianist.

Linda coached the girls that Beethoven needed to be fixed at the vet. She explained that he had started to watch the birds and other creatures out the window. By having "Ludwig" neutered, she reasoned that his desires to roam and wander away would lessen.

During spring break from school, the Burkholder family brought their young Beethoven to the veterinarian to have his "snip job" (neutering). The check-in and procedure were completed with no complications. Their home was just ten blocks from the vet clinic. They all waited in anticipation for the phone call to report the successful surgery and recovery. At the end of the day, three little girls and their mother came to take Beethoven home. No pet carrier was used, just the snuggling of him under the jacket of one of the daughters was required.

* * * *

Oh, happy day. That is, daylight hours anyway.

Mid-evening, the phone rang on my library study desk. The clinic answering service reported a distressed dog with a fishhook in his lip. I returned the call and set out to the clinic to meet a chagrined fisherman dog owner. Sure enough, the dog had chowed down on the baited end of a fishhook and the barbs were embedded in its upper lip.

A late spring mist dripped on the fisherman, his dog, and me as we met in the parking lot of the veterinary clinic. I noted a meowing in the dark alley, which seemed to be coming from the adjacent, abandoned warehouse. Now, fishhooks stuck in a lip of a dog look like a minor inconvenience but removing them can be just as tricky as getting one out of a fisherman's finger or the mouth of a large-mouth bass. A light anesthetic is used to relieve any pain incurred in the operation. Specific surgical instruments—side cutters from the shop tool collection—are used to cut the hook in half. Then gripping the remaining hook shaft with the needle nose pliers, the barbed end is easily pushed on through the lip to be removed from the outside. Another successful surgery—or could it have been described as, "catch and release" or, "bait and switch." The limp, sleeping body of the big dog-fish was scooped up and carried to the back seat of the SUV to recover from sedation at home.

Shutting the door of the SUV, I heard the sound of meowing again. That distinct, distressed sound came from across the alley. I reached into my pickup to grab a flashlight to explore. I was never one to ignore a feline SOS call. The mist illuminated a wet, broken window and the silhouette of an adolescent cat perched under the protected sill. Reaching down to pet and greet the little kitty, I was immediately drawn by its familiarity. I had just seen this kitty earlier in the day.

Taking him back into the clinic, I inspected the collar with a heart-shaped tag. Sure enough, the mystery was solved. It read "Ludwig."

No way, I mused, but a quick phone call to the Burkholder house confirmed that Beethoven had, indeed, escaped out the back door and run down the alley earlier that evening. He had been missing ever since. I waited for Linda and the three girls to arrive to rescue this elusive Alley Cat.

After school ended in May, Dr. Burkholder remarried and accepted a job in Illinois. It was a bittersweet moment when I handed them Beethoven's—aka Alley Cat's—records and bid them godspeed. They drove away into the sunset from the vet clinic. I never heard from the family again, though this amazing cat and its love for adventure and music will long be remembered.

Blue Eyes Oliver

Ode to
Blue Eyes Oliver

His deep blue eyes resembled Sinatra.
Yowling at night, sounded like opera.
This Big Oliver just drifted into town.
Where he came from, never was found.

Roamed farm to farm along Sage Road.
Slept in barns, sheds, and any abode.
Stopped by to eat at many back doors.
Took to the vet for his cat fight sores.

Kept farmers company while milking the cows,
Followed them daily as they fed the sows.
Even rode the tractor when baling the hay.
His offspring started coming, with his easygoing way.

One night in the city, met Phoebe the kitty.
Preferred the tuna, not this pretty little bitty.
But nine weeks later, six kittens she bore.
Oliver the blue eyes is known in the lore.

No one ever knew what happed to the cream-colored cat.
Disappeared one night and never came back.
His genes in neighborhood are carried by many.
Loved by farmers, wives, and families aplenty.

ike Jimmy Dean's "Big Bad John" *who just drifted into town and stayed alone*, Oliver the blue-eyed tomcat did the same. Maybe he did not work in a mine, but this handsome, cream-colored stud became a neighborhood friend of the farm families along Sage Road. He appeared randomly at backdoors while cleaning himself from his latest battle with another territorial gladiator cat.

Neighboring farmers Jerry, Steve, and Marlyn, all somewhat stoic in character, often spotted Oliver, as the tomcat came to be known. These three men had been childhood friends who went to a one-room schoolhouse together. They attended the same rural Mt. Hope Methodist Church and belonged to the same 4-H Club as youth. They grew up to live on their family farms, though outside work helped provide a means of income for each of them. Each confessed to talking to Oliver as he followed them around while they attended to their morning chores in the sheep and calf barns.

Oliver was not the least bit wild, and for a tomcat, he was very trusting. He rubbed his body on their blue denim pant legs and was rewarded with pets and conversation with these men. Their rough, weathered hands did not seem to offend him. The farm wives, children, and visiting grandchildren all became attached and enamored of this blue-eyed cat.

Farmer Steve had just finished the last swath in the knee-high alfalfa field. He mowed this rich, purple-flowered legume with a sickle pulled behind his tricycle-style, classic Oliver tractor with its narrow two front tires. The power takeoff rotated the sickle blade as it slithered along at ground level laying the mowed hay down in a perfect carpet path behind. As the glowing orange orb of sun set at the horizon, it silhouetted the tractor's return to the farmstead. In the June twilight, the single beacon tractor headlight penetrated the silent layers of dust from the recent passing of a car along the gravel road. Steve parked the tractor under the row of elm trees for the night. He turned the key to the off position, dismounted, and remembered to place a coffee can over the upright vertical exhaust manifold to prevent any moisture from getting into the engine. His dawn to dusk day had started with the milking of twenty cows, feeding sheep, and finishing the mowing of the hay. When he walked toward the house for his late supper, the fragrance of the crabapple blossoms welcomed him home.

A farmer never has to set an alarm, as their internal switch makes them rise early for chores. The Holsteins had already gathered at the barn door for milking. Farmer Steve flipped on the predawn barn lights, delivered scoops of ground corn and meal ration to the front of each stanchion, and opened the gate to allow the eager cows in. Each cow knew its stall and rushed and pushed to eat their morning feed. This hour and a half of milking and cleanup was repeated every twelve hours, every day of the year. As Steve left the barn that morning, heading back for his own breakfast, he glanced to the side and sensed he was not alone. A tail was dangling below the yellow tractor seat that he had parked the night before. Stepping up onto the hitch, he found a cream-colored cat stretched across the soft, well-worn tractor seat. He reached across and rubbed the cat's chin with the outside of his index finger.

"So, you found a warm spot to spend the night, did you? I've seen you darting across the road a few times, and here you are." Steve visited with the sleepy-eyed cat as it stood and stretched, shaking off the slumber. "Well, I can always use some company, and I hope to see you around if you choose. I guess I'll just call you Oliver, as the old tractor is my friend, too."

The name Oliver stuck, and the tomcat's deep blue eyes became legend on Sage Road.

It did not take long before there were farm kittens resembling Oliver, at least his tender, gentle personality. A litter from a tortoiseshell queen was born in a basket in the sheep barn. She had five kittens—none of them cream colored, but with Oliver's demeanor and good posture.

One of the neighbor women worked at my veterinary clinic. Oliver accompanied her on the eighteen-mile commute in a pet carrier several times a year. We performed emergency care to treat a draining abscess or swollen eye from his latest battle for supremacy over the Sage Road harem. African tigers, lions, or cheetahs can be described as having prides or clusters of felines. Oliver's kingdom was much larger, and his enjoyment in spreading his love from farm to farm became renowned.

A morning phone ringing in the kitchen, a window rolled down with neighbors visiting along the road, and a conversation at church often included the question, "Have you seen Oliver lately?"

"No, I really haven't," or "Yes, he was by our place for dinner just a few nights ago," were often the answers. "Yep, that cat is something. I've never seen one like him," or "I'm not much for cats, but he is a neat one, isn't he?"

24

Oliver's bite wounds were never too serious. To defend themselves in fights, cats use claws and teeth latch onto their opponent's ears, face, and body—wherever the jousting match allows a male cat to grab on and inflict damage. A bite wound by a cat is known to be the second most contaminating bite of any animal. (The most infectious bite just happens to be *Homo sapiens*—human.)

Visits to the vet to have such wounds treated doubled as an opportunity to bathe, deworm, and give Oliver a few nights in town for "rest and recovery." His blue eyes attracted all the hospital staff. He was a big hit as he rubbed and preened on them while they cared for his latest owies.

There developed an admiration society when Oliver looked into the faces of his caretakers and tilted his head, giving his raspy meow, seeming to say, *Thank you so much for the petting and attention, but would you mind giving me just a little more of that canned tuna?*

A typical tomcat develops thickened, tough skin around the head and neck from fights with marauding males, or even from spats with females during the mating act. Oliver had a blocky head but managed to avoid wrestler's "cauliflower ears." (The ears of cats and a 125-pound wrestler are remarkably similar.) If a blood vessel or capillary is ruptured from a sharp blow or a canine tooth, it will bleed, serum seal, and cause a hematoma. Left untreated, it forms a perfect incubator for infection. The very fragile ear, which is nothing but cartilage covered by a soft layer of skin, becomes scarred and misshaped from the drainage and surgical repairs.

Handsome Oliver avoided such ear damage or scars. He was able to duck the savage "left hook" by his opponent tomcats' claws or the snarling bites to the ears. Even his many scratches over the forehead healed without leaving a blemish. The hair always grew back and did not disfigure his broad face.

If cats can smile, Oliver was such a guy. His story of planned parenthood at the home of a veterinarian was one he could share at the "feline retirement home" years later, or at the neighborhood cat-gossip party. You see, my daughter had an exceptionally prissy kitty named Phoebe. She was beyond beautiful, to put it in boy-girl, human vernacular. As maturity, or adulthood, comes to all cute little kittens, so it did for Phoebe. Sure enough, her posturing and incessant guttural meowing and carrying around stuffed animals in her mouth were dead ringers, clues that this poor little kitty needed a partner. As a strictly indoor cat, there was no opportunity for a random, outdoor male cat to father her kittens.

Wait, but what about Oliver? After several bouts of Phoebe being "in season," the meowing and stuffed animal parades and threats from the vet's wife that she was going to take Phoebe to another vet to have her spayed if he did not do something, a plan was hatched for Oliver to get a night on the town. On one of his freeloader trips to have a battle injury patched up, he was slipped out the back door of the vet clinic to meet Phoebe for a one-nighter.

The plot was set. Oliver was sneaked into the house by the back stairs. Probably unsteady from rocking back and forth in the unfamiliar confinement of the pet carrier, he sauntered out when the door was open, did his cat stretching thing, and took a 360 to scope out his surroundings. He had entered a quiet, clean basement with boxes, a refrigerator, counters, and Christmas decorations stacked away in the corners. Not quite a barn setting, and Oliver guessed right away that this was a city dwelling.

Surprise! Here was a full dish of canned tuna. He was smitten. Tuna was his favorite. While he began snarfing the fresh morsels, the door was again cracked open, and the most feminine beauty was scooted in and the door closed behind her. Phoebe hissed and the hackles on her neck accented her arched back. Then she began growling, *What in heaven's name is this cat doing in my house!*

Now, even though Phoebe was definitely in full estrous, she was not up to this match-making scene. *He's a country bumpkin, no matter how nice looking his deep blue eyes.*

Oliver showed absolutely no interest in Phoebe, or at least he was more enamored by the cuisine paté in the China dish. As the hissy little cat approached him, Oliver ignored her, wincing finally when she came face to face. Oliver glanced to his right, while licking his lips, only to be belted by the two front paws of this little meowing, snarling, and all-teeth-exposed beauty.

If it had been a boxing ring, Oliver would have been on the canvas with this barrage of lefts and rights to the chops. It was like the last ten seconds of a welterweight fight, where only one of the fighters is throwing punches. Oliver stood his ground, having seen a lot of battles, but being swatted by none other than a declawed little tortoiseshell just didn't seem fair. Unfazed, he lowered his head for another bite of tuna. Phoebe backed up and seemed satisfied that she had stated her case. There was no way for any romance or extracurricular activities.

After this night in the basement, and hoping for some more male-female interaction, Oliver climbed into the pet taxi for a return trip back across town to the vet's office. He slept most of the day, only lifting his head when a kennel attendant passed to check on him and the other animals. At the end of the day, his ride took him back to his Sage Road kingdom. Who knows where cats hang out, or if they ever have a show-and-tell, or even a few bedtime stories with other cats. But Oliver's unsuccessful night with the little city cat, Phoebe, would surely be requested as a "tell it again" story by the feline harem.

One day, Oliver, much like "Big Bad John," drifted out of town and never returned. The farm neighbors inquired and even had random search parties organized to look for him along the roadsides and cornrows. But Oliver was never to be seen again. His genes are still passed along in these neighborhood farms, decades later. The debonair, cream colored, blue-eyed tomcat lives on in the memories of many.

Boss Cat

Ode to
Boss Cat

Having only one eye, this black and white tuff,
Left for dead along the English Channel bluff.
Found by three sisters, on the way home from the beach,
Was covered with ticks and even a leech.

Staggering to walk, he followed them home.
Their Mum said, "We can't leave him alone."
So off to the vet, carried him in a box.
By the looks of his wounds, had fought with a fox.

Their dog Sparky, all cats he did hate,
But this one was special and became his mate.
Won over the family, Boss Cat was the name.
Chased off other dogs, if into his yard they came.

Before long off the porch and allowed into the house,
Dad said he was a keeper after catching a mouse.
Boss Cat slept with the girls and hogged the bed.
He loved marmalade and cheese on his bread.

Played with a canary and caught goldfish in pond.
Craved chocolate whirlies, he was quite fond.
On Dad's evening walks with Boss Cat at heel.
On a stool at the table, his manners unreal.

Reginald Edwards was an orphan and found himself in Egypt at the age of sixteen dodging the bullets of the "Desert Fox," Erwin Rommel. Following the war, he returned to England, married, resided in Peacehaven, and worked in the Defense Department in London which was an hour's commute. With his wife, Maggie, mother-in-law Nana, and three daughters, he lived along the Channel in a cluster of eight houses that perched on the cliff's edge.

A stout, black and white cat terrorized the alleys and back doors of the small shops in the village. Dogs, cats, and even seagulls allowed him a wide path and were no match for his cunning claws and razor teeth. He scavenged and was known by the locals as a hunter of small rodents, bunnies, and rats that he found in the rocks and crevices of the white cliffs below Peacehaven. He thrived off handouts and leftovers from numerous loving backdoor neighbors along the streets and alleys. The villagers held him in high esteem as he would be seen dragging an oversized dead rat down the alley with his head extended high so as not to step on the lifeless body with its corrugated gray tail.

The girls' mum had some firm rules but still allowed them freedom and independence to explore their neighborhood and all the magnificent white cliffs over the beach at Sussex. A family rule was: when playing on the ocean's edge, the time of high tide had to be noted and taken into account.

Each day their grandmother, Nana, packed a lunch for the girls as they left home and descended the 188 Bastion Steps to the sand. The sisters wandered and played along the white beach. Christine and her two younger sisters dressed in long, white lace dresses and picked their way through the seashells and ubiquitous seaweed washed up in the last high tide. Nana loved to provide these dresses for the girls for everyday and for play clothes. Seeing them playing in the waves with their seaweed jewelry braided around their heads, necks, and wrists brought her joy.

One day, a sudden storm chased the Edwards girls from the sandy beaches below. The tide was coming in as the three girls watched the dark clouds with white billowing tops approaching from

31

the south. With only a few minutes to spare, the little dirty seaweed queens in their muddy, white lace dresses crawled over the chalky incline for home. The beaches started to empty as the time for neap tide approached. With the salty spitting wind leaving a film of coating on the shoreline, the trek back up the bastion steps was done in bits and starts. Each landing along the switch backs allowed for a rest for the old and young alike. Out of breath at the top of the steps, the trio trudged along the chalky incline path. They reached their back porch just as the hurricane-like winds and horizontal sheets of tadpole-sized rain pellets began buffeting the windows of their home.

Reg was not home from his train commute as the three girls, Mum, and Nana huddled in the front room, watching the branches and debris skip across the front yard like feathers in a breeze. They listened to the whistling of the wind through the trees, and then heard an eerie ripping sound from overhead. There was a crash on the roof. Peeking out the front window, they could see that part of the roof had broken free and was tumbling and buffeting across the yard. It pounded and flipped like a dying bird as it came to rest in the backyard of the butcher shop.

After what seemed like an hour, the gale force straight winds began to subside. The girls were given permission to venture out in their galoshes to assess the storm damage. A rainbow had appeared in the north as the angry, white, cumulous clouds atop the dark bench cloud below began to dissolve. The peaceful, full arch of the rainbow with its band of seven distinct colors was a welcomed sight after the storm. The girls waded in the puddles as water cascaded down the gutters. They investigated the shattered roof and fallen branches and matted leaves stuck to the houses.

Mum stepped out the front door to see the neighbor lady across the road sweeping her waterlogged stoop. They exchanged looks and a few words. Mum was not in the least happy when the lady told her that a cat had "bashed" on her door during the storm. She was aghast, in fact, that the cat had been left out to survive on its own through the mayhem. Mum Edwards enlisted and dispatched the three girls to see if they could find the cat.

The girls ran across the debris-littered cliff tops. In a large, natural crater lined with scraggly rocks and shrubs on the path down to the beach steps, they spotted a motionless animal lying under a thicket. Stepping over the boulders, they discovered the cat was in a desperate way. It was the scruffy, one-eyed black and white kitty lying motionless. He was covered with ticks and looked up as the girls approached. He had wounds on his head. His neck was crusted over with dried blood and sand.

down to touch him. It was like the Good Samaritan

s | trail and had passed the struggling animal, doing

n | look like you have been in quite a battle. We don't

h | llow us, we'll sneak you some goodies."

t of the depression to the path above. He meowed

an |

lkway to their back door. They bounced into the

ho | warmed a cloth and gently massaged a few of the

op | emed to brighten after a time of enticement with

sar |

id. Much to the delight of the girls, Mum picked

him | eterinarian. The kind doctor with gray, thick bushy

eye | the tomcat looked like he had been in a fight with

a fo | ıld be put to sleep?" he casually mulled.

uggested, "Just do your best to clean his wounds. He is

com | g home with us."

The Edwards girls and their mum carried the box with their new adoptee home. The black and white cat met face to face with their dog, Sparky, who had been rescued several years earlier. Sparky was very protective of his territory but, miraculously, greeted this beat-up old kitty with its pitifully mauled face and legs with friendliness. The dog carefully started licking at the kitty's face and ears. The old fighter had been chased by every dog in his world, but this dog was somehow a different mate. The cat crawled out of the box, stretched with his front feet reaching forward, and Sparky led him over to his own bowl of food and let him eat all of it.

Christine looked on in amazement. Sparky had chased every cat that ever crossed his path prior to this. "We shall name you, Boss Cat," she said with a giggle and a wink. The name Boss Cat stuck, and this thin, hungry cat took over the back porch.

There had never been a cat allowed in the Edwards home before Boss Cat. Their father, Reg, had been adamant that all cats should be on rodent patrol, and that meant outside.

A box was cut down, and Boss Cat was laid inside on the porch to lick his wounds.

"But what is Daddy going to say?" asked Christine.

Mum answered. "This cat is on a journey, and we'll let him continue that journey. If he stays a few days to recover, we will help him along."

The plan was soon abandoned as the black and white cat awakened and sauntered into the washroom. Reg arrived home and shook his head at the amazing damage done to their house by the storm. Stepping onto the back porch, he threw his hat on the bench, only to see a resemblance of a cat in streetfighter's makeup. The girls knew this was against the rules and they whispered to Mum that Daddy said the cat must go.

"You let me handle this," Mum said, as she confidently headed back to the family quarters to find Reg hunched over, petting the cat's chin with the back side of his index finger. She stood in the shadow of the doorway and heard him mumbling, "Well, old fella, you look like you could use a few days of fixing up and loving."

Mum knew that he had been touched, and this old Boss Cat was to be part of the family.

Reg took Sparky on walks every evening on the cliff tops with no leash. Sparky had been abused prior to coming to live with the Edwards family and was not interested in people. Any time a broom was taken out of the closet, he would growl and head under the bed. On their walks, Sparky was all over the place—sniffing, running, and exploring the rocky ridge. Boss Cat was soon invited to join them on their jaunts and walked at Reg's heels the whole way.

Reg often said, "It is bloody embarrassing. Here I am walking along with a cat at my heels. When people pass and say good evening, I know they are laughing under their breath, because my dog is nowhere to be seen by then."

Nana lived next door with a gate between the houses. The gate was always open. On one occasion, it had been shut, and it completely upset Boss Cat as he had to walk around the houses to get home. He had a full run of Nana's house, as well. He loved fishing for goldfish in the pond in her garden, though he was only lucky once.

Nana purchased the girls a full-size pram from a rummage sale. Before Boss Cat, the girls would fill it with their dolls and parade up and down the street. But now, Boss Cat became the main attraction as he wore a baby cap and, covered with a blanket, he appeared to be napping. A lady at the butcher shop asked to see the baby in the pram. She was quite shocked, but the girls acted like it was normal to have a cat dressed up in a stroller. They proceeded to laugh and giggle all the way home with the story for Mum and Nana.

Boss Cat was a food junkie. Marmalade, shrimp, mussels, and Curly Wurly bars. At Nana's house anything was possible. A favorite was winkles. Nana gave the girls a bucket and said, "Winkles, please? Now, nice and full, off you go, watch out for the tide." (Winkles are a snail-like shellfish.)

Boss Cat was always available for testing any food. He was very adept at hooking a shrimp out of the bucket. It did not faze him when Nana told him, in her great London accent, "You are nothing but a thief!" She never swore but used her grand vocabulary in talking to him. Boss Cat was not able to steal mussels or winkles very well with his paws.

He was able to hear the crinkle of paper three rooms away. The wrapper of the Curly Wurly, a popular English candy bar, brought the cat darting like a cheetah for his favorite chocolate bar. If one of the girls had taken just one small bite, Boss Cat perched himself on the arm of the chair and ate the rest quite neatly. No crumbs of chocolate or toffee were left on the chair. It was just nibble, nibble, nibble, all the way down. The smell of the Curly Wurly seemed to penetrate the walls, even from outside.

At sister Rita's birthday, twelve little kids sat at the dining room table with their party hats and small sandwiches. Boss Cat sat at the table, too, on his stool. He had a plate but did not eat off the dining table. He patiently sat next to a small child who was in awe of this one-eyed cat. He played up to the tots, and the attention egged him on. From that day forward, he sat on his stool at the dinner table while the family ate. His head moved from side to side, often tilting it as he seemed to ponder who would speak next. He loved to be at the family dinner table and started pacing in the kitchen when the oven and stove were wafting delightful aromas. No meal was complete without this rough tumbler sitting on his throne.

Mum had become the recipient of a canary, left to her in an old lady's will. Peppy was a golden yellow bird and was quite pretty. "I have no one with whom to leave him, Maggie," Blanche Cartwright confided. Blanche just knew that Mum, with her great love of animals, would look after her pet. The day finally came when Peppy and his cage moved into the Edwards home. A constant battle ensued between Boss Cat and Mum to keep Peppy safe from harm. Boss Cat had arrived in the home *after* Peppy, and he loved to sit staring at the fluttering canary with the eye of a hunter ready for pouncing on prey. He was able to hook Peppy out of his cage, once even without having the door open. After the hooking feat, Peppy was moved to the kitchen so that door could be shut between them at night.

Boss Cat seemed to know the time of day as he sauntered up the main road to meet the girls walking home from school. He never crossed the main road but sat patiently to see the skipping little girls with their lunch pails come home each day, wearing their print dresses. Some days he would wait in the dip along the roadside, intensely planning the next hunting capture. The kids' noises, running, and doing kid-crazy games seemed to annoy him. It spoiled his hunt.

When Reg and Maggie started a cleaning business, the Edwards family, with Nana, moved to an acreage southwest to Cornwall. Boss Cat was let out of the car at parks and rest areas. He was never on a leash and had a great time in the forest. He crouched in attack mode to chase the young foals in the pasture. The mares were not at all pleased and stomped their feet and came charging toward Boss Cat with their teeth bared and ears back. Boss Cat would leap back and sprint at full speed to jump in the open back door of the car. While the whole family laughed, Reg said, "Well, old puss cat, those old mares just don't know how to have fun."

The new acreage had a barn, pigsty, and stables. It came with four barn cats. Boss Cat quickly established the pecking order. When the girls became older, and Christine entered college, it freed up one bedroom. Boss Cat slept every night on the bed. He finally had a room to himself. On holidays and visits, he seemed almost indignant that he had to share a bed again.

Little girls grow up, leave home, and occasionally visit on holiday. Letters from Mum and Nana were a treat, and each one included the latest antics of Boss Cat and Sparky. After college, Christine took a job in Switzerland at a hotel doing event planning. She managed seventeen banquet rooms and conventions that were full most months of the year. She received a letter that Sparky died peacefully in his sleep and shed tears as the memories of the pup adopting Boss Cat flooded her mind.

A year later, while vacationing and backpacking in Thailand, a letter arrived in Bangkok from Reg. He so seldom ever wrote, and Christine carefully opened the flap on the envelope.

My Dear Little Seaweed Queen,
I regret to inform you that our dear Boss Cat has succumbed today, October 17. It is exactly one year to the day that dear Sparky slipped away.

We love you,
Reg

Cookie

$1650

Ode to Cookie

With kitten in arms, in her tight fittin' jeans.
In a turquoise shirt, she looked like a queen.
Sold Cookie the cougar, but didn't come with
The buyer was smitten if you catch the drift.

Utilities meter was read by a lady
Wanted to pet this cute little baby.
Didn't know he was playing, with her hand in his mouth
Pulling back was scratched, things quickly went south.

Cookie's new home, was a crib built for corn
He daddied six cubs, were cesarean born.
Cookie kept one eye open overlooking the crew.
Shena and Tabitha, became mother cats too.

One day when buffalos were unloaded.
A few minutes later, the boards all exploded.
Ralphie the bull, ran with great haste
A desperate posse lit out for the chase.

Ron talked to the animals and walked the walk.
The "whisperer" he was while the peacocks squawked.
Zebras, llamas, goats, and donkeys all together
Cared for and sheltered in all kinds of weather.

Marlin Perkins and "Mutual of Omaha's Wild Kingdom" aired from 1963 until 1988, bringing exotic animal stories from Africa and South America into the living rooms of television viewers. A cadre of animal lovers became enamored and dreamed of having these animals on their own farms and preserves.

Each spring and fall, the Lolli Brothers Livestock Market in Macon, Missouri, drew crowds from many surrounding states. These exotic animal enthusiasts had two things in common—they loved animals and considered themselves disciples of Marlin Perkins.

In Central Iowa, a University of Iowa graduate, Ron Dornath, landed his first job. His dream of a backyard full of a variety of animals was spawned. Ron had been raised on a farm with White Embden geese and ducks. One of his family's many endeavors was to dress and sell these birds for the dinner table.

Ron purchased an acreage along busy US Highway 218. The farm had a two-story house, a barn, and a modest stable for horses. A horse and buggy accompanied the purchase. Ron's first acquisitions were not necessarily exotic. A donkey, Sicilian burros, pygmy goats, and a peacock came to his new barnyard. He walked among them, hand-feeding and talking to each one in his gentle "Marlin Perkins" manner. Geese and black swans floated gracefully in a concrete-bottom pond with flowering lily pads.

Another enthusiast, Clarence Scribner, became a good friend and mentor to Ron. Clarence's own collection of animals included buffalo and elk. Llamas in his fenced yard along Highway 63 caused passing motorists to do double-takes and crane their necks as they passed. Clarence invited Ron to join him in his motorhome and drive to Missouri for the Lolli Brothers Exotic Animal Sale.

The sale pavilion was packed with a crowd wearing cowboy hats, bib overalls, tight fitting jeans, and baseball caps. They sat on tiered, wooden benches. The Show-Me State drawl and fine-looking women added to the flavor of the arena. When the sale began, the auctioneers fired up the crowd. Into the sale ring came one interesting animal after another. There were camels, giraffes, kangaroos, llamas, bighorn sheep, buffalo, and finally, a four-month-old cougar cub.

Anyone who has ever attended an auction knows that the one rule is to never make eye contact with a spotter. Remain stoic, don't nod the head or wiggle a finger or thumb. The exhilaration of bidding often causes even the most rational and practical people to get caught up in the drama and forget about the dollar amount of the bidding.

Ron had followed the rules through the afternoon. Then it happened. The cougar kitten was carried into the ring. It was starry-eyed. It had gorgeous blond fur accented with dark spots on its face. It was cradled in the arms of a pretty "Ellie Mae" type beauty who could cause even a nearsighted person with trifocals to pay attention.

After some hype by the auctioneer, the bidding began. Ron fell into an almost hypnotic trance as he raised his hand. The thrill of the chase and drama of the quick, back-and-forth bidding allowed no time to rationalize the spending involved. Starting at $300, this little kitten had at least four bidders. When the bids reached $1,000, several bidders backed off. The auctioneer's staccato pumping egged on the remaining hands. Ron stayed in the bidding against an old Missouri codger who only winked his bid, never moving another muscle. The auctioneer's voice slowed, and he finally offered, "Going once, going twice, and sold to the man there in the Hawkeye hat for $1,650."

Ron had no idea that his ride in a friend's motorhome would end with him writing a big check for a young cougar. This was the easiest part of the purchase. Questions spun in his mind. "Can I hold him all 200 miles home? Does he need a cage? What do I feed him? Is he as tame as this pretty blonde made him out to be?"

With the bill-of-sale in hand, Ron walked back to the holding pen area behind the sale barn. He saw the blonde in her turquoise, cowgirl shirt surrounded by a few admirers. He approached pen number twenty-two. The girl was still holding Ron's little kitten.

He introduced himself and showed her the bill of sale. With his slow drawl, he pried for tips about caring for the cougar. Miss "Ellie Mae" followed him to the RV and handed the kitten off to Ron. Ron said, "I guess I should ask! Does he have a name?"

"Well, I call him Kookie. I know it sounds crazy, but I always loved Edd 'Kookie' Burns [of *77 Sunset Strip* fame—*Kookie, lend me your comb*, the song lyrics rang], and with his beautiful hair, that's what I called him. But, of course, you may call him anything you want."

Kookie's name was modified to Cookie as he crossed the state line into Iowa that night. He was embarking on a life that would extend past his thirteenth birthday.

40

Cookie's daytime playpen became a small, galvanized corncrib which had been used for ear corn many years before. A sturdy four-inch square wire fence around the circumference, a cone shaped, solid tin roof, and a concrete base made a perfect den. Cookie sat on a perch mounted on an old tree trunk in the cage to observe the other animals in his new kingdom. A braying donkey, screeching peacock, whinnying horse, and constant squawk-squawking geese were all neighbors in his new home.

"Well, good morning, Cookie. Oh, what a stretch! It's time you wake up. You'll like this special meat this morning," came Ron's greetings at dawn.

Sitting high on the tree truck, Cookie had a front row seat to all the activities at the farmyard. When a dusty livestock trailer backed into the yard on a Sunday afternoon, Cookie nattered as it backed up to the side of the coral. An unusual smell was coming from inside and a deep bellowing sound was heard. The back gate to the trailer was dropped and out darted two burley, huge, curly-haired beasts. Buffalo! Then the excitement began.

The horse pen, which seemed so high and sturdy, suddenly started shaking and bowing outward. There was the sound of a crash, and the largest buffalo, Ralphie, scaled the fence and knocked off the top two boards. He was running straight towards Cookie's crib, pounding the dirt with his hooves. The aluminum gate at the entrance to the paddock proved no stronger that a matchstick. The brute crashed through it without stopping to take names.

The rodeo was on. Ralphie was heading "hell bent for election" right up the middle of the busy two-lane highway. The two delivery men and Ron headed up the posse in hot pursuit. A double decker semi coming at a fast speed saw the scene, like out of the Wild West, and braked while blowing his air horn. The noise got Ralphie's attention, and he hung a right at Dunkerton Road heading due east. Men running on foot are no match for something with four-hoof-drive. What they were going to do if they caught up with Ralphie did not seem to cross their minds.

At the railroad tracks, Ralphie veered into the ditch and was soon out of sight. Out of breath, the slightly overweight and out-of-shape pursuers stopped to catch their breath and formulate a plan. After this two-mile chase, they conferred and decided that they needed horses to head off this big, thousand-pound relic of history. Short of calling on Buffalo Bill, they decided to wait until Monday morning to bring horses and track Ralphie down with a dart tranquilizer gun.

The rescue of the great escapee would never see the light of day.

At dusk, as Ron pulled into his driveway, he received a phone call reporting the sighting of a wandering buffalo at the crossroads of C-57 and Leversee Road. Before he could get the pickup turned around, a police car with red lights flashing streaked by with its siren blaring. Ron considered the worst and followed the racing squad car. As the truck crested the hill, it looked like a police car reunion with red flashes lighting up the evening sky. Stopping along the gravel pull-out driveway, Ron could see a car upside down in the ditch. Still fearing the worst, Ron moved closer and found that a teenager had hit something in the road. The car was turned upside down, but thankfully the driver had walked away unscathed. Ron came forward and asked what he had collided with. "It was a bull or something. It is over in the other ditch. I think it's dead," the shaking young boy blurted. Sure enough, Ralphie was laid flat out like he had taken a direct hit in the side and died instantly.

What is one to do with a huge animal on a Sunday night along a county road ditch? The wrecker called to the scene for the car helped to lift Ralphie by his back legs and drop him into Ron's pickup truck. Ron knew that the locker in Clarksville had a reputation for processing exotics. With the help of the men who had delivered the buffalos that afternoon, contact was made, and Ron drove the deceased thirty miles to the locker that night to be ground into buffalo burger. His plans of just a few hours earlier, to have a breeding herd of these large burly ruminants, was derailed for the time being.

On a sunny day about a month later, a utilities meter lady made a call to the farm to read the water meter. She asked Ron if she could pet Cookie. Even though Cookie was just playing, his mouth closed around the lady's arm, and she panicked. In pulling her arm away, Cookie's fang canine tooth scratched the skin. It was utility department policy to report any animal bites. Because these were almost always dog bites, the report of a cougar bite brought the police onto the case. Ron was required to install a six-foot high, chain link fence around his property to protect his animals from escaping and the public from inadvertently encountering them. This fence proved expensive, but it did keep the buffalos "home on the range."

A female cougar, Sheba, was purchased when Cookie turned two years old. They became soul mates and chased each other in play every day. It did not take long before Sheba was showing a rounded tummy, obviously pregnant. She took over the corncrib den and Cookie was moved to an adjacent den.

The phone rang at my office on a cool summer evening. "Hello, this is Dr. Kenyon. How can I help you?"

"Hello, Doc. This is Ron Dornath. I am not sure what I have gotten myself into. As I told you last week, Sheba is pregnant. She started labor this afternoon and has had only one cub so far. She seems to be straining but nothing comes out. Could you come out and see if she has one blocking the birth canal?" he pleaded.

To say that Ron was laid back and never showed excitement or angst would be an understatement. "She's out here in the crib. I have rigged up a spotlight if you need it," he offered, matter-of-factly.

And there she was, a 130-pound cat laying on a mattress, her retinas glowing red in the bright light. I knelt a few feet away. "Sheba, Sheba, Sheba," I softly called to her. "I can't say I've ever been an OB for a cougar before, so we will work at this together," I mumbled, trying to get a visual assessment of her condition.

With the little kitten nudging at Sheba's underside, looking for a faucet, I asked Ron if he could hold her head for me. With a caressing headlock, Ron snuggled her in his arms and assured me that he had her. I do not know if I was totally trusting, but I proceeded to clean Sheba with the warm soapy water from a pail. A vaginal exam revealed nothing was in the birth canal. All this maneuvering was done with this cat growling a steady musical gurgle, telling me that she did not appreciate my presence and the pressure on her. Palpating the abdomen, I felt some hard, round bodies as I held my hands on the lateral sides.

"Jeez, Ron. There are more in there. She must have uterine inertia. While I could give her some oxytocin to see if that would move the fetuses down, there's a risk with that. I can't touch anything in the canal. If she had uterine torsion, that could be fatal. What do you think about me doing a cesarean?"

Ron calmly replied, "If that is what you think, Doc. Let's do it. Just tell me what to do."

Cookie paced back and forth in the cage next to Sheba's birthing crib. He seemed to be surveying my every move, and an occasional deep-throated, rumbling growl made his presence known to us as we worked on Sheba's dystocia.

An injectable anesthetic was given in the leg muscle. In less than an hour, there were six live baby cougars laying under the heat light. The surgery had been very routine, and the sutures were well placed in the uterine horn. With Ron relaxing his hug around Sheba's neck I said, "These skin sutures will dissolve, so there will be no need for me to come back to take them out. The incision line here should be watched for redness or any drainage around it. I have given her a shot of long-acting penicillin, so there will be no need for you to give her any medicine. These babies all seem full-term, and they do not show any side effects from the anesthesia to Sheba. They may be a little sedated from the Ketamine anesthetic, but it should fully wear off in about an hour."

From his adjoining cage, Cookie had stopped growling and stared at the kittens trying to nurse. He watched their every movement.

Four of Sheba and Cookie's kittens lived to adulthood. Two of them were sold to interested parties. Two of the females, Tabatha and Shena, matured; and each had a litter of kittens themselves. Regulations on having wild animals as pets became more stringent and the market for cougars dried up, meaning it became exceedingly difficult to sell cougar kittens.

Ron never married; however, he had many female admirers who loved his cougars. Cookie was always their favorite. He usually laid on the couch and listened to television. These houseguests could hug him, and he often went to sleep in their arms. He lived for thirteen years and never sired another litter of kittens. These wild kingdom collections of animals were put under surveillance of the Iowa Department of Agriculture for inspection of animals' health and housing. Ron's kingdom was a stellar example of good animal care.

Cricket

Ode to Cricket

Born in a chicken house, out on a farm.
Rescued by a lady with loads of charm.
Chattering and chirping noises from his throat came.
'Twas cause of this, Cricket became the name.

When the lights went off, into bed he came.
This bouncy kitten right in the face of the dame.
Sentenced to a carrier, but soon loved this nest.
At last, Mama and Papa were able to rest.

Tethered outside to a stake on the lawn.
To bugs, and fluttering butterflies was drawn.
"Cat on hot tin roof," maybe not quite.
This one slept atop the stove, o'er the pilot light.

Developed a problem which caused to 'upchuck'
Allergies they say, was cured with peas and duck.
When he smiled, showed his clean white teeth.
Brushed them daily, his rewards were fish treats.

Marla grew up in the small town of Manchester, Iowa. Her parents had separate businesses along Main Street. She worked for years as a salesclerk at her father's shoe store after school and on weekends. Sales and customer interaction and satisfaction were in her blood. Marla, petite and pretty, was barely five feet tall. Her porcelain soft complexion, dancing blue eyes, and smile accented her bubbly personality. She was a perfect fit for the children's shoe department.

Her mother's retail store was adjacent to her father's shoe store. Seeing both parents run businesses, manage employees, and juggle inventory gave Marla an incredible background in business and dealing with people. In high school, she did not have a boyfriend as most boys were not as mature and work oriented as Marla.

Following high school, Marla moved to a nearby college town. She found a job at the local, upscale Von Maur department store. There was no on-the-job training necessary, as her years of work at her father's store provided the skills she needed for this new job.

Marla found an apartment in the lower level of a two-story, white clapboard house in a 1920s neighborhood built around the college after the First World War. The large front porch had a suspended swing and faced a boulevard lined with flowering crabapple trees. Marla moved in, prepared to live a quiet, restful life with her cat, Missy. When she was not working or sleeping, she was cleaning and singing to her favorite music on the radio.

One Saturday morning in late May, she heard the click of her mailbox at the front door. She went to the screen to see a handsome young mailman adjusting his letter bag. He had reached the bottom step, on his way to continue his mail delivery route, when he heard the door open. He was immediately entranced.

"Good morning, Ma'am," Ted the postman said with a smile as he doffed his blue cap.

Marla blushed and giggled. "Oh, hello there. Thank you for the letter. It is the first mail that I have gotten since I moved in, Mr. Postman."

"You are welcome, and you can call me Ted. It's my pleasure." The postman smiled and winked.

This morning exchange between Marla and Ted the postman turned into a daily occurrence. Marla would sit on the porch swing and look forward to this innocent flirting. By the second week, they had become comfortable. Shy Ted said, "I probably shouldn't do this, so this is off the record. Would you be interested in going out for supper and a dance this Saturday?"

Marla answered, "I'd love too, though I have to work until the store closes at six o'clock."

"That's no problem, because I have to deliver mail on Saturday and won't be off until five myself," Ted said.

Their first supper date at Rolinger's Restaurant was punctuated with laughter. They were comfortable sharing with each other about their upbringings, families, interests, and jobs. They discovered that music and dancing were mutual enjoyments. The evening passed rapidly with non-stop chattering and laughing, including a trip to Newberry's for a special ice cream dessert in a waffle cone. They held hands as Ted walked Marla back to her apartment. They agreed that the next date would be a square dance the following Saturday.

Square dancing in the United States became popular entertainment in the postwar 1940s. Western-style square dance was complete with the ladies in cancans and garters and men in boots and snap-button cowboy shirts. The caller—with his rhythmic, nasal-toned, Gene-Autry-style voice—issued commands to the dancers through a microphone—bow to your partner, join hands, single file, pass through, star, find your partner, promenade, and do-si-do.

Back at home, Marla greeted Missy, her longhaired, calico princess. Did Marla detect a bit of jealousy? She consoled and petted her lovely cat, assuring her that Ted would not take Missy's place in her heart. There was room enough for both of them.

When Ted arrived to pick up Marla for their second date, Missy hissed and darted away. Marla did her best to coax the cat out from her hiding place, but Missy clearly wanted nothing to do with the intruder.

The unhappy cat forgotten at home, Ted and Marla swooned in each other's arms as they square danced with their friends at the Electric Park Ballroom.

A whirlwind courtship was followed by a wedding six months later.

There was only one glitch. Missy! The cat resented, disliked, and flat-out hated Ted. There was nothing he could do to earn her forgiveness. When Ted moved in, Missy declared war. Each night, Missy started peeing on Ted's side of the bed. No amount of disciplining, scolding, or psychological reasoning made matters better. The blankets, sheets, and mattress were soiled and stained.

Marla's frustrations found no end until a new home was found for Missy with an elderly lady. Missy was content to have her own person. She didn't want to share.

Ted's work for the post office continued, and he was transferred to the nearby Waverly office. The newlyweds eventually moved to Janesville and Sam, a rangy black rescue cat from the humane society, soon became a member of the family.

Sam was an aloof cat and not a real lover. He slept by the fireplace, ate any food in his bowl, and patrolled the house, quiet as a mouse. Before Marla knew it, ten years of peaceful co-existence with Sam had passed by. Marla heard about a litter of five farm kittens that desperately needed a home. Encouraged by a co-worker, she went to see them. On her car ride to the farm, Marla had a premonition that a new kitten was in her future. How would she choose? Such a random selection, yet one look and the coal black kitten latched on to her heart. It made a unique purring sound. Sitting on her lap on the ride home, the kitten got his name.

"You twitter just like a cricket. So how about I call you Cricket?" Marla said to the black furball coiled on her lap.

Cricket's chirping was a lifelong characteristic. He chirped continually as she walked around Marla and Ted's house. While perched on the windowsill bird watching, he chirped. While playing with a ball, he chirped. When Marla came home from work, Cricket followed her around the house, talking and chirping.

Thankfully, Sam took one look at Cricket, the new kitten, and ambled away, indifferent.

Marla was nervous the first time she brought Cricket to see me, his first visit to the vet. He chattered amiably on the ten-mile trip to town. However, as soon as Cricket was taken out of his carrier, he stopped being a friendly kitten. He assumed a Halloween scary-cat stance and turned into a feline possessed. Instead of twittering and chirping, he let out an evil, yowling cry.

I had barely had a chance to meet him, much less examine him. Marla was so embarrassed by his behavior that she repeatedly scolded, "Cricket! Cricket! This is not called for. He hasn't even done anything to you!"

No amount of cajoling and "nice kitty" stuff worked in calming Cricket.

"Please get me a warm towel, and we'll see if we can get him out of his defensive posture," I said to my veterinary technician. With Cricket somewhat constrained under a large, terrycloth towel, I found an open spot to slip a needle into this little black demon. It didn't seem fair for such a sweet little lady to have such an ornery patient. Thankfully, Cricket only expressed this side of his personality at the veterinary clinic.

One Monday morning, an urgent call came into the clinic and my receptionist answered. She brought me the phone. "Doctor, Marla is on the phone, and she sounds very frustrated. Could you visit with her now?"

"Sure . . . Hello Marla. Good morning, I hope? How can I help you?"

"Oh, Dr. Kenyon. It's my Cricket. He is driving me crazy. He's the love of my life, but I can't get any sleep." Marla sounded out of breath. She was clearly frustrated.

I pulled up a desk chair, sensing that this was not going to be a brief conversation. "Okay, what seems to be the problem?"

"Well, I've told you how Cricket follows me everywhere from room to room all day. His chattering seems almost like he's talking to me. I love him to death. But now when we go to bed, he wants to be right up in my face, wanting to play. I can't push him away. He acts like he *needs* to be with me and will not quiet down. What am I going to do? I love him so much!"

"Marla—hold on. Time out. This little rascal loves you too. But somewhere here we need to set some boundaries. Why don't you try putting him in a carrier at bedtime? You could start by having the carrier at your side of the bed. If he yowls in protest, move it to the far side of the house. What do you think?" I offered as a first step in search of the solution.

Marla did not hesitate, "I think that sounds great. I can't go on any more nights without sleep. He just seems to want to be near me. Ted sleeps through it and doesn't even know what is going on."

I had not heard from her for about two weeks when I was called to the retail wing of the vet clinic to visit with Marla, who was purchasing some cat food. I moved quickly through the clinic to meet her, fearing what I may hear.

Marla greeted me with a huge smile. "Oh, Dr. Kenyon, you are a genius! Ever since we've started putting Cricket in a carrier at night, he's a new cat. He seems to like it, and he sleeps through the night right on my side of the bed. I can't believe it. He even paws at the cage door when we head for bed. I just can't thank you enough, Dr. Kenyon!"

I smiled and accepted Marla's gratitude, relieved that Cricket had redeemed himself. "Well, that's great. I'm so happy this worked. I only hope he's not looking forward to his next traumatic trip to see me. I'm sure his behavior here last time was just an aberration." I smiled at Marla, and maybe my fingers were crossed behind my back.

Marla trained Cricket to lead with a collar and leash. He was the center of attention as neighbors watched him, staked in the front yard to a swivel screwed into the lawn. Marla sat under an umbrella in the shade in a lawn chair while watching him. There was not an insect or crawling bug safe within reach of Cricket's tether. He stared for minutes with his head tilted, ears erect, and only an occasional twitch of his tail. Then with a pounce he would trap the millipede or chinch bug with a well-placed paw. Butterflies fascinated him, as they were attracted to the milkweeds in the garden. He would reach up with his paw to tap the stalk to see the Monarchs' wings open and close as they sat on the flowers.

** **

Why do animals seem to be attracted to people who least want them? Cricket could pick out the type in a lineup. If a stranger visited that fit the bill, Cricket was at their feet, weaving on the inside and then the outside of their legs. One such person was Marla's mother. She had not allowed any pets in her home when her two daughters were growing up. And now, her own flesh and blood had cats on the table, the couch, and sometimes on top of the stove!

"It's time to brush your teeth, Cricket," Marla would call, and down from the cat perch leaped Cricket at a full gallop. He would jump up onto the sink ledge. Special, poultry-flavored toothpaste was applied to the tiny head of a brush. First one side was brushed and then the next. Cricket licked his lips and waited for the special double-enzymatic action, CET freeze-dried fish treat. He sat up in praying stance, anticipating this fish morsel dental treat. As his veterinarian, I was never able to thoroughly examine his ivories, but his breath always smelled fishy clean.

Cricket found the top of the stove by accident while he was trying to reach for the fish treats. With two gas burners on each side of the stovetop, he walked onto and plopped down on the center island porcelain plate that covered the pilot light. The pilot heated the plate and became his favorite sleeping place. What a strange scene for Marla's mother to see. She loathed and abhorred the fact that the cat was allowed in the kitchen, much less on the stove where food was prepared. Such admonition did not prevent Cricket from seeking this warm siesta spot.

❄ ❄❄

I noted on the appointment calendar that Cricket, with owner Marla, was coming in that afternoon with a vomiting problem. I feared this would be another rodeo.

Upon entering the exam room, I wanted this experience to be different than recent annual examinations and vaccination sessions. Reading the faces of clients often gave away their concerns before they had time to ask questions. Today proved one of those times.

"Hello, Marla, and you too, Cricket. I see on the record that he has been having some vomiting problems. How about we just leave him in his carrier while we visit to get some history of this issue?"

I asked all the usual questions. "How long and how often has this problem been going on?" "What does the vomitus look like?" "Is there any hair in it?" "Blood?" How long after eating does it happen?" "Does he seem to be having normal BMs?" I questioned and listened to the concerned woman's answers.

She explained that it started happening once a week or so and had increased to every time that cat attempted to eat. The food was coming back up, looking almost exactly as it did going in. No color change. No hair. And Marla had begun to expect that Cricket was losing weight.

"I have put his food in the blender and pureed it, and still the same results. I have tried different brands of food: Science Diet, Iams, and all the hairball cat foods. They seem to work for a few days, and then it starts all over again."

Marla was worried that it might be cancer. She was frantic at the idea of losing her Cricket.

"First, let's examine him thoroughly. I will take his carrier dome top off, and I will slide this plastic box over him, giving him a short inhaling gas anesthesia so that he will relax for a better evaluation of his body." Acting quickly, the top was off the carrier, the chamber was secured, and the isoflurane-oxygen gas mixture began to fill the chamber. Convinced that Cricket was "out like a light," the technician withdrew a blood sample from the jugular vein. I massaged and deeply palpated the abdomen and stomach. I confirmed the heart and lungs were clear and the lymph

52

nodes and throat were all within normal limits. The mouth and tongue showed no abnormalities. X-rays of the thorax and abdomen were taken. Within ten minutes, Cricket was awake and chattering back to us as he lay in his carrier. This had been a much smoother exam than all of his previous visits.

The question remained. Why was Cricket vomiting? I sent this asocial cat and his concerned owner home with the promise to review the x-rays and blood work and give Marla a call in a few hours.

There are a few flow charts for vomiting cats that help to eliminate potential causes. Every diagnostic test we ran showed no abnormalities. The physical exam had been uneventful. The x-ray showed roughened edges in the stomach, but no sign of occlusion, growths, or blockages. Following the flow cart to the bottom arrow gave me a list of some obscure types of organ changes as possibilities. There was the little-diagnosed food allergy with an asterisk at the bottom. The note stated that this is an exceedingly rare condition. But it was something to hang a hat on and I thought it worth a try.

Hypoallergenic diets are offered with novel and unusual protein sources, along with carbohydrates that are not found in any cat commercial foods. I chose rabbit and peas for Cricket.

"Hello, Marla." I bravely managed to greet her using my most convincing voice. "I have some particularly good news. Cricket's organ systems are all very normal, and I have not found any problems on the x-ray. With your descriptions of his vomiting patterns, I believe he has developed an allergy to some of the foods that he is eating," I paused to let this information be understood.

"That is all well and good, but what are we going to do about the allergy?" she said.

"I can't be certain, but I would like to try him on a special food, one that he has not had before. We call it a novel protein carbohydrate diet. I am suggesting either a rabbit and peas diet or another one is duck and peas. I have them both on hand if you are willing to try them," I offered.

"Dr. Kenyon, this is wonderful. I thought surely you were going to find something bad. If it's just an allergy, this sounds fixable, doesn't it?" Marla asked, sounding hopeful and happy.

"Cricket is a special cat. No cavities and fresh breath. Now let's just hope he has rabbit foot's luck, and this solves his problem," I said with conviction.

Genius—I'll take that title if it works. Luck—It is always welcomed. And a special chirping cat needed help. Together, Marla, Cricket, and I shared many more years of friendship.

The Maine Coon Breed

Genetic Selection and Reproduction in Cats

Abraham begat Isaac; Isaac begat Jacob; and Jacob begat Judas . . . for fourteen generations until . . . *Jesse begat David . . . David the king begat Solomon . . . Solomon begat Roboam . . . about the time they were carried away to Babylon . . .* for fourteen generations until . . . *Joseph* . . . and the birth of Jesus.

Matthew (KJV)

And so it was in biblical generations. It would be eighteen centuries before Charles Darwin—the theologian, medical student, world traveler on the *Beagle*, philosopher, and scientist—wrote the first of six editions of *The Origin of the Species.* Tracking the evolution of a species is a slippery slope; and in a cat's heritage, it is not possible at the present time.

Genealogy for humans can be traced through bibles, archives, written history, and even DNA tracing. Various theories exist on the origin of a Maine Coon cat, but there is only one constant denominator—Maine. This rocky coastline of the most northeastern state was a close location to the New World for European navigators. Vikings and Scandinavians may have been the earliest to land on these shores. Cats were aboard ships to control rats and mice. One theory as to the origin of the Maine Coon is that a Norwegian Forest Cat may have gotten ashore and mated with feral mainland cats of the area.

The Turkish Angora longhair breed was prized by royalty in France. Those cats were traced to a rescue ship trying to bring Marie Antoinette out of France to escape from the Revolution in the late 1700s. The ship was waiting off the French shore loaded with all her belongings when she was nabbed along with Louis XVI and guillotined by Robespierre. The ship, captained by Samuel Clough, did sail with all these smuggled possessions, sympathizers, and six Turkish Angora cats. It landed at Wiscasset, Maine, where Clough's wife awaited. Did some of these Turkish Angoras interbreed with the domestic Maine cats of that time?

Another theory is that a sea Captain, Charles Coon, who carried big cats aboard his ship to control the rats, may have brought some of these longhaired buccaneer cats ashore. With the last name of Coon, he is an intriguing link to the Maine Coon Cat's origin legend.

Regardless of where it came from, this big cat with its unique characteristics has evolved and is credited to the state of Maine. They are long-haired cats with tufts of hair between the paws, hair in the ears, polydactyly, a long and narrow face, and they tend to wash and dip their food like a raccoon or bear. They can sit on their back feet like a squirrel holding a nut. They run like dogs and are remarkable hunters.

The term *polydactyl* means extra toes or digits. A six-toed cat is an anomaly in the United States. The extra digits are found on all paws, but primarily on the front paws, usually between the first and second toe. This genetic mutation has spread through some cat populations, especially along the Eastern seaboard states. Ernest Hemingway had a love for polydactyl cats. Though they do not look like the Maine Coons, more than fifty of these cats can be seen meandering around the Hemingway house and courtyard at Key West, Florida.

I am from a farm in far Western Kansas and graduated from Kansas State University Veterinary College. We had many cats on the farm, often exceeding two-dozen outdoor kitties. I even had one exceptionally rare, male, gorgeous tri-colored calico. In my youth and in my days as a young veterinarian, breeds of cats were unheard of, with the exception of an occasional Siamese brought into the university clinic. A cattery was a foreign concept. People didn't breed cats; cats took care of that business on their own. What we knew about feline genetics was that calico (having hair with three colors of black, orange, and white) was a sex-linked gene, which meant they were nearly 100% female. The male calico was extremely rare. Growing up, I was very naïve and had never heard of the Maine Coon Cat, much less of an extra-toed feline.

I was first exposed to polydactyl cats in Ashland, Massachusetts, where I worked at a veterinary clinic. Of course, every owner of such extra-toed cats, which were products of their neighbor's litters or from adoptions at pet stores and humane shelters, thought that their special cat was a Maine Coon. None of these domestic cats had any of the other special traits of the breed. This may have been explained by genetic drift, or the centuries of out-crossing of many generations of wild and feral cat populations. With Massachusetts being so near Maine geographically, it certainly seemed feasible that outbreeding may have been the reason for seeing the polydactyly coming from Maine feral cats.

Erick the Red

Ode to Erick the Red

Erick the Red just a cat from Maine.
At Madison Square, he found his fame.
At this show, turned many a head,
Lost in Manhattan under a bed.

Washed his food with paws every day.
Came from afar, for his kittens to pay.
Gorgeous red hair, cream undercoat too,
Tufts in his feet and his genes were true.

Enjoyed a harem of ten beautiful queens.
Cattery living for this tom, a reproductive machine.
With the run of the house, whenever desired.
Purred like a kitten, when others admired.

Two & a half feet, from the nose to the tail.
Known for his beauty, this debonair male.
Constipation plagued him, more fiber he got.
Slept in a condo, his owners had bought.

To the cat Hall of Fame, a star was made.
This gentle giant, goodbye to friends bade.
From the Land of Lincoln, to NYC
Archived in history, his DNA would be.

In my forty years of veterinary practice in Illinois and Iowa, polydactyl cats and kittens were seen only a few times a year. So, I was surprised when Kathryn Thompson stopped at the vet clinic to ask me about Maine Coon Cats. She informed me that she was going to purchase one. We lived in a university town. There were different and interesting professors located here from all over the country. Kathryn and her husband Dave had met at Bowdoin College in Maine, and then taught at the Western Illinois University. They had no children. Recently, they had attended a cat show in Peoria, Illinois. Cat shows attract unique feline enthusiasts who share their passions for their breeds. The Thompsons were drawn to the Maine Coon exhibitors and visited at length with the breeders. They caught the bug to purchase one of these cats, and they were attracted to a brown and white Maine Coon named Klaadin's Candi, which they ended up purchasing from the Harper Valley Maine Cattery in Indianapolis.

Candi had emerald-colored eyes, thick silver hair, and a darker, mahogany undercoat. She was outgoing and purred when petted. Her movements were fluid and the long, silver-colored bushy tail flagged as she pranced. The ear tufts and the tan colored hair between her foot pads fit the description of a perfect specimen of the Maine Coon breed. Per the contract when purchasing her, she had to be spayed and not allowed to reproduce. She was a great first cat for the Thompson's home, and they jumped right into the cat show circuit in the altered division. This opened the door to the establishment of the Maine Coon Cattery in Macomb, Illinois, in the basement of the David and Kathryn Thompson's home. Candi, their first Maine Coon, enjoyed a long life there.

For a breeding program, it logically takes both sexes. The Thompson's purchased a stunning red male named Kennebunk's Olafson from Portland, Maine. Olaf sired Babar, so named because when he stood, he had an arched back like the renowned show elephant. This black smokie's registered name was Babar Olafson.

At cat shows, Babar drew crowds. His incredible smoky-gray undercoat was a marvel to spectators. At shows, judges use peacock plumes or feathers to draw a cat's attention. They move in certain ways, tantalizing or teasing a cat to move its head and eyes to show off its facial features.

At a show in the Quad Cities of Illinois/Iowa, the peacock feather became the prey. Babar reached up and grabbed the wand with his big black paws, broke it in half and kept it in his possession. The wise judge did not try to retrieve it.

Maines behave more like dogs at a show. They are gentle giants and seem to enjoy the pageantry. No growling, clawing, or biting a judge. Male Maines top out at fifteen to eighteen pounds. If they ever show aggression, it may come from jealousy.

Meanwhile, locally, the Thompson's Cattery grew to seven large, condo-style kennels for the toms. They were complete with climbing posts, platforms with constructed jungle gyms, and protected, elevated hutches for privacy and sleeping. The queens had free roam on the floor of the basement with each one having her own open-doored, private hutch.

As noted earlier, Maines have distinct personalities. They wash all their food, dipping it in a water bowl. They then hold it with their hands, much like a raccoon. They rarely drink water, preferring to dip their paws and lick from them. Placing water bowls in a three-story condo usually ends with the floor wet and the bowl empty. Attempts to outmaneuver this habit, by placing the water bowls in large Rubbermaid tubs, also usually ends with the bowl empty and the plastic tub holding the water.

"David, we have to figure out a way that the water is not always emptied all over the floor," demanded Kathryn.

David had done all the construction of the kennel cages and had another idea. "How about some of those water bottles with the gerbil type spigots?" The next week, seven gerbil waterers were attached to the cages.

So, you think that is going to work, do you? This is going to be a game, the observing cats thought as the bottles were installed. Sure enough, the cats could empty them in thirty seconds. The toms would place a paw on the spigot and watch proudly as the water flowed onto the tile floor.

More cats were purchased from Maine, Illinois, and Georgia. Through contacts at cat shows and phone conversations, the Thompsons saw many distinct colors and characteristics.

(Attention, Reader: What follows might be considered risqué. If this offends you, just skip the next two paragraphs!)

Dreams of running a successful cattery require reproduction, or introduction of the males to the females. The novice may wonder if the cats are up to this event. Matchmaking and worry of the potential commotion are soon put to rest. It seems that these instincts run wild, even though this new indoor environment may be foreign.

With the queens on the floor, only one tomcat was allowed out of the condo to mate, "and so it was in the beginning." The first litter of kittens brought a whole new meaning to being in the cat business. In only sixty-three days after mating, five wiggling, four-inch-long kittens are all pushing for a spot at mom's dinner plates. Birthing in a special bed, in a quiet nursery, allowed for periodic viewing. An observation consistent with every litter born to David and Kathryn's Maine Coon Cats in the next twenty years was that at day three, after birth, the mother would move the kittens. She carefully picked each one up with her mouth by the scruff of the neck and moved them to a new bed with a clean towel. Speculation as to why the mothers do this is to get the litter away from all the newborn smells. This may be an instinct to distract any attention from stray cats or predators.

At twelve weeks of age, two of the first litter were spoken for by another university professor and her husband. Kathryn tried to expound on every do and don't for these first-time cat owners. She nervously gave them all the records and a food and toy care package. She thought she had answered all their questions until the phone rang the next morning.

"Mrs. Thompson, this is Dr. Rose. I have one thing to share that you did not tell me. We put the kittens in the bathroom overnight like you suggested. We put the water dish right next to the food bowl as you said that they may want to dip their food in the water."

"Yes, that all is correct. Did you have problems?" Kathryn asked, curious about their concern.

"Well, you did not tell us to put the toilet lid down, and they must have used their paws and have actually emptied all the water in the toilet. They filled it with the roll of toilet paper and a shredded box of Kleenex," Dr. Rose said as she laughed.

This was the last time any kittens were sent from the Thompson Cattery without this warning of toilet training for the new owner.

* * * *

The phone rang as the veterinary office opened on a Monday morning. An exasperated voice said, "I need to speak with Dr. Jim!"

"Hello, this is Dr. Kenyon. How may I help you?"

"Dr. Jim, I have a problem and concern," Kathryn said. "I was at a show yesterday and learned there is a syndrome in Maine catteries they are calling a heart disease, maybe hyper-myocardiopathy or something like that. Have you heard of it? I am worried my Felicia has it. She has all the symptoms they were talking about: shortness of breath, occasional open mouth breathing, and I think she is losing weight, too."

"Now, hold your horses. You know, when you get a bunch of breeders together at a show, the rumors and stories fly. Let's not jump to pull the alarm. Bring her in and I will examine her." I was a relatively young doctor at the time, but I had learned the importance of calming a worried client.

That morning Felicia the Maine Coon came to see me. She had, indeed, lost weight since her last examination. Her hair was unkempt and oily. She had a distressed look in her golden yellow eyes. Upon examination and auscultation of the heart and lungs, I sighed. I had hoped Kathryn's worries could be dismissed.

"Kathryn, I know you just heard of this syndrome of hyper-myocardiopathy (HCM). It means that the left ventricle of the heart chamber is thickening. The heart is losing the ability to pump the blood efficiently. Felicia's heart rate is indeed more rapid than it should be. You mentioned that she is panting occasionally? This could also mean that she is trying to get more blood or oxygen uptake to the rest of her body more rapidly. I suggest we take an x-ray here to see the extent of the heart enlargement. To truly get a better picture, I will need to refer her to the University of Illinois Veterinary Hospital to get an echocardiogram. That's the best outcome that I can tell you at this time."

"How much time does she have? And what in heaven's name am I do with her littermates that have already been sold?" Kathryn asked. Devastation showed on her face. She thought she had been doing everything correctly by checking the genetics of every cat she purchased. Thankfully, she had painstakingly recorded each breeding and was going to be able to trace back the cat that may have brought this heart problem to the cattery. Each of Felicia's littermates were returned, one new owner was from as far away as Texas. The owners were given the option of choosing another kitten or getting their money back. The returned littermates were all examined, and none showed HCM symptoms, but were all altered to prevent any further spread of the syndrome.

❉ ❉ ❉

David had become enamored by Red Maine Coons while he was showing at his first cat show. He checked with a breeder of Reds from Georgia. After visiting with the cattery owner, he flew to Halstead Airport in Atlanta and purchased Erick the Red. Flying home with a young cat under the seat of the airplane is not an easy task. A meowing and worrying cat can distract the other passengers. "Shhh you little Red, and we will make our connection and get home by dinnertime," David pleaded with the cat. Erick was a great traveler and not a peep was heard.

"Oh, David, he is everything you said he was," Kathryn exclaimed. "He will be the foundation of our breeding program and put us on the map."

Within eight months, Erick's first kittens were ready for placement. They carried the beautiful, parallel, darker red stripes down their backs and the distinguished swirling heart patterns on their shoulders.

Cat shows throughout the Midwest were opportunities for the couple to display their Maines. Erick had indeed put this Illinois cattery on the map, and the demand for his kittens soared. Erick and Babar had both won Best of Show at qualifying events and were invited to show at the National Cat Show at Madison Square Garden. Driving a van with two cats in the back was no small thing, and flying to New York City with two cats was an even bigger challenge.

They hired a college girl to stay at the house and manage the feeding and care of the cattery. With Erick and Babar in separate carriers, the Thompsons boarded a plane at the Quad Cities and flew to the Big Apple. Neither of them had been to New York before, much less toting two cats in a pet carrier.

Kathryn's mother had made a cover for the carrier and embroidered the words "Erick and Babar Olafson—Lincolnland Maines" on the side flaps. With all the regulations and arrangements, it was possible to put both cats in the same carrier. Erick and Babar were very compatible and rode on the plane, bus, and subway like seasoned travelers. When the United flight from Chicago landed at LaGuardia, they caught the bus to 42nd Street on a sunny and perfect "Chamber of Commerce Day" in the big city. Streets were lined with taxis and delivery trucks in the inside lanes, and the honking was incessant. They took the subway and arrived at the famed Macy's. The Renaissance Hotel at Midtown was an easy walk from there, even with the heavy cat carrier in tote. The two cats had learned to balance in the carrier and not move around and rock the boat.

Erick and Babar sniffed out the seventh-floor room. The carpet was a wonderfully deep, blue nap which made stretching and digging their claws rhythmically a pleasing motion. It looked like they were playing a piano.

The atmosphere at Madison Square Garden was like no other the Thompsons and the cats had ever experienced. There were 385 entries from all over the United States and Canada. Erick was the runner-up in his class of forty-eight Maine Coons. The judging drama came down to Erick and a silver Maine from upstate Ithaca. At the last minute, the ribbon for the best of class was placed on the New York cat, qualifying it for the final round of Best of Show.

Both Erick and Babar had been troopers with their charming personalities, showing off for all the competitors, spectators, and judges.

This was a storybook trip to New York—a dream for the Thompsons, until . . .

❋ ❋ ❋

Back at LaGuardia for the return flight check-in, the security guard requested a look under the cover of the pet carrier. He lifted the shroud and said, "Yes, there is one cat in there."

Kathryn, stunned, said, "One cat? No, there are two cats! See?" She bent down to show the agent, but to her shock, only Babar was in the carrier. She exploded. "David! You were the one who put the cats in the carrier. Where is Erick?"

Poor David was on the hot seat. He scrambled to retrace the morning's events and remembered that he did latch the door to the carrier thinking that the two cats had already walked in on their own. Wrong!

"Alright, don't panic. Erick has to be back in the hotel room hiding somewhere. We have a small window of time here, but let me backtrack our commute. I will hurry and fetch Erick," he pleaded, hoping for an understanding wife.

The concierge directed David back to the scene of the disappearance. Running around the maids' laundry carts on the seventh floor, he unlocked the door, and the search for the elusive cat commenced. Finally, after calling his name repeatedly, the skirt of the bed was lifted and out came the proud Maine Coon, runner-up champion—Erick, the Red.

Fatima

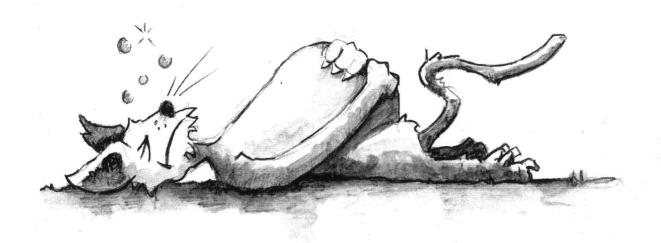

Ode to Fatima

Kansas City Kitty, that is what she was.
Became Annie's love, a warm ball of fuzz.
A tortoiseshell kitten, Fatima by name.
Out the window at nights, a hunter became.

Motherhood happened at least twice a year.
Eighteen litters, always a tomcat near.
Found homes for seventy without even an ad.
In the Village, word of mouth the household had.

Came and went as she pleased, but always came back.
Brought mice and lizards for the kittens to snack.
'Twas hit by a car and nearly died.
Placed in rehab, where mother nature revived.

To the family's condo, she moved to Vail.
Hunting continued, squinnies and voles on the trail.
Ate too many and a blockage evolved.
Fifty miles to Leadville, where the vet resolved.

Shared her home with a dog named Lassie.
This tricolored cat and the poodle were classy.
Little girls grow older, and to college depart.
Fatima was saddened, died of a broken heart.

Little Ann was five years old when her mother gave her permission to get a kitten. She found one in nearby Mission Hills. "Oh, a coat of many colors," she said upon seeing the kitten. This pretty, six-week-old feline came to live with her for the next thirteen years. The Kansas City tortoiseshell kitty paraded with a distinction of beauty and style. The kitten was named Fatima, a name plagiarized from Ann's Texas cousin's Siamese cat.

Her little girl bedroom was on the second floor of a sprawling, Frank Lloyd Wright- style home with the country club abutting the backyard. Oaks and maples shaded the mid-century, modern home. Squirrels dropped acorns like grenades from the overhanging branches. Possums, raccoons, mice, and ground squirrels populated the savannah in the backyard. Fatima loved it, and would stalk the wildlife, freezing at the sight of any moving creature. Her pensive yellow eyes seemed to land like lasers on even the twitch of a squirrel whisker. If looks could kill, Fatima would have cleared the backyard of this rodent cousin. The squirrels would chatter until they sensed her eyes were fixed on them. A game of cat-and-squirrel could last for hours.

By the time Fatima was six-months old, the open window of Ann's bedroom was the cat's secret escape into the world of nature outside. Squeezing through the opening, she balanced along the narrow railing, hopped down on a sloping two-by-six board, and jumped to the ground below. Freedom.

Where she went, who she met, what she caught, and how she survived the marauding tomcats and raccoons will never be known. By the crack of dawn, she was always lying snuggled next to her little girl companion.

Ann's brother Mark, who was one year younger, only wanted a dog, and not just any dog. He had been glued to the television, and he wanted one like Lassie—a brilliant, smart collie dog who starred in adventures and rescues with her little boy. Mark's mother started searching for a collie to meet the wants of her four-year-old son. Finding Fatima for his sister had been a snap. She even broadened her search to look for miniature collies called shelties.

Fatima had been a family hit. Mark's begging for a dog amplified.

Mark's mother finally located a litter of puppies in nearby Lawrence. She and Mark drove thirty miles to the address and found the curly haired, black puppies. One of them was more outgoing and licked Mark's face. The boy was careful not to reveal his doubt that this was a collie dog. As the trio drove home, holding the puppy in his arms, finally he blurted it out. "Mom, this isn't a collie, is it?"

"No honey, I believe this is a poodle. But I'll keep looking for a collie for you. They have been impossible to find," his mother confided.

And so it was that a black poodle named Lassie came to live in Kansas City with Fatima the tortoiseshell cat. The neighbors could all hear the family calling from the backdoor, "Lassie, Lassie! Come home!"

The curly-haired, ungroomed poodle would come running from the woods, just like the television Lassie.

❈ ❈ ❈ ❈

Somewhere around kitten litter number nine or ten, the family had moved to Vail, Colorado, where Ann's father was an internal medicine doctor at Vail Medical Center.

Once again, from the condo bedroom window, Fatima tapped the glass with her foot to get her freedom into the outdoor woods. The prey had changed, but the hunter instinct had not. Chipmunks, mountain voles, and mice were ubiquitous. She proudly dragged them, dead or alive, back through Ann's bedroom window. Fatima gave lessons to all the new litters of kittens. They learned, first-hand, the taste, smells, and skills of hunting and procuring food.

Ann's father had worked late at the Medical Clinic one evening and arrived home to a distressed adolescent girl.

"Something's wrong with 'Tima," she cried.

Fatima laid groaning on the carpet with a distended abdomen. She could not be pregnant because she was still nursing. "Oh, Annie. I am fearful that she may have an intestinal blockage," replied her father after palpating the cat's tummy. The three of them hurried to climb into the blue Caprice station wagon and set off to the nearest veterinarian in Leadville. They drove over fifty miles through the mountains on a clear January night. The vet's office was in his home, and he answered the late-night call. He was ready for them when they arrived with the moaning, big-bellied Fatima.

"Oh kitty, you do have a problem," he said out loud as he examined Fatima. "You know Doc, as you said over the phone, she definitely is clogged up," the small-town, cowboy-looking, country vet surmised. "Is she a hunter by any chance? And does she eat her catch?"

"Yes, she is a fanatic poacher," the MD father answered.

The scruffy-bearded vet thought and finally suggested, "I am going to give her a soapy enema with a touch of mineral oil and see if I can break down this wad of fur, bones, or whatever is stopping her up."

After a third infusion rectally of the warm solution, small chunks of bones, fur, and remnants of an overindulgence of wildlife started coming out of Fatima's bottom end. The midnight ride home with the moon casting shadows through the aspens was a pleasant respite for Fatima, who was wrapped in a towel in Ann's arms.

* * * *

'Tima's adventures at night did bring out the boys. Just like clockwork, sixty-three days after a tryst with a stranger each spring and fall, a litter of three, four, and even five kittens was born in a cardboard box-bed in Ann's closet. The excitement and news of each birth brought neighborhood children to hold, snuggle, and love the adorable little furballs. Ann's mother had only one unbendable rule. No one could come to visit the kittens until their eyes were open at about ten days of age.

One litter after another came. Black ones, white ones, tortoiseshell, yellow, cream, tabbies, and grays. Much like the childhood Sunday school song, "Red and yellow, black and white, they are precious in His sight," Fatima's kittens displayed the spectrum of diversity.

After litter number seventeen, Ann's mother took Fatima to the vet to have her spayed. To everyone's amazement, she was pregnant again. Fatima dodged the bullet one more time, but after the eighteenth litter, the surgery did take her out of the kitten business.

Finding homes for over seventy kittens was actually never a problem. Fatima was adamant that none of the stragglers were welcomed to stay in the home and live full time. No advertisement except word of mouth brought adopting families out of the woodwork for a now-famous Fatima kitten.

During her reproductive life, Fatima never missed a meal. She came home every night. But then it happened, one night Fatima was crossing the dark street in the rain and a speeding teenager hit the brakes and slid to a stop on the blacktop. Hearing the screeching tires, Ann's family rushed out thinking an automobile accident had occurred in front of their house. There, sprawled on the wet street, was their little multicolored kitty. They carefully scooted her onto a square of plywood and set off to the nearby veterinary office. The vet on call met them and assessed Fatima's condition. "Well, considering I see no tire marks, she may have just been rolled under the car. That is better than being run over by a tire," said Dr. Gage, a middle-aged, mustached veterinarian. He examined the limbs for fractures. The chest and lungs sounded congested, but no broken ribs were noted. "She may have internal injuries. A concussion is more likely the cause of her weakness and being laterally recumbent. How about she stay with me tonight, and I'll give her some supportive care. We'll see if she responds." the vet suggested.

The next morning, Ann and her family were called back to Dr. Gage's office. He reported on Fatima's condition. The x-rays had shown no fractures. Fatima's yellow eyes looked up at Ann as if to say, *"I'm sorry, I shouldn't have been out on the street on a rainy night."*

Dr. Gage, a family friend, suggested taking Fatima home and confining her in a quiet, warm, and dark room. He hoped the concussion and traumatic bruising would respond. Sure enough, on day three, there was scratching at the door. When opened, out came Fatima, trying to maneuver the steps to come down to the kitchen for her food bowl and water. This traumatic experience did not curtail the nightly escapes into the wild blue yonder from the little girl's bedroom window.

❋ ❋ ❋ ❋

The day came for Ann to enroll at the University of Kansas. When moving day arrived, the family station wagon backed down the driveway, and there was Fatima peering out of the second story bedroom window. With tears welling in her eyes, Ann waved goodbye and blew her cat a kiss. She lamented, "You know Dad, for thirteen years, we have never been separated, except when I went to camp. Will you love her for me each night?" she asked.

Her dad was touched emotionally as he backed into the street. Choking down a lump in his throat. He nodded and said, "You know I will."

A few weeks passed and Ann received a call at her sorority house. "Ann, it's Dad. I have to tell you that Fatima died last night, here on your bed. She had been so quiet lately. I can only think that she died of a broken heart without you."

Reproduction 101

"Repro" is a curricular section taught to all aspiring veterinarians and agriculture majors. A brief introduction to the beginning of life for a cat may give one an appreciation. To most humans who have never witnessed the birth of a kitten, or seen a queen preen and care for her babies, this scene is for you. The instantaneous miracle of a mother of any species with her wet offspring emerging from a birth canal is heavenly. Imagining the pain of delivery from a male's perspective is impossible to comprehend, though seeing the ecstasy on the new mother's face is undeniable.

Baby kittens are rather unattractive for their first twelve days of life. How they find a nipple is entirely instinctive. It is almost like radar. Emerging wet and steamy into life, they are licked incessantly by their mother. This nourishing massage by their mother's barbed and roughened tongue stimulates blood flow through this little creature poking around her belly. There is not a set number of baby kittens in a litter, but the most consistent average is four.

Cats normally are a seasonally polyestrous species. This means that their estrous cycle is timed by the winter and summer solstice. As the length of the day changes, in late winter and early fall, the ovarian release of estrogen starts to change in a cat. Tomcats can smell a female queen in heat from alleys, blocks, or even farms away. Funny how that works! There may be more species that are stimulated like a feline, but outside of rabbits, the list we know about in detail is small. A cat will continue to stay in heat, or receptive to a male cat (tom), until the actual mating occurs.

At night, the sound of a tomcat yowling and fighting and battling with other toms is news that there is a female cat involved. The "fight on the Serengeti" ensues in the pursuit of this queen. Though these battles are numerous, the actual skirmish is evidenced by few. A victorious tom will have as many battle marks as a middleweight wrestler. Cauliflower ears, scratch marks across the forehead, bites on the neck, back end, and tail make the typical quaint, country scene seem like a war zone. There must be an instinctive ecstasy of the final pursuit that drives even the least aggressive tom's testosterone.

The flirting queen is no less vocal and tempting. Though trying to fend off such a pursuit may seem like a faint attempt, the use of claws, biting, and eerie guttural yowling punctuates the night air. The actual event lasts no more than ten seconds. "Thank you, madam," the male bites the neck of the female, holds on for dear life, and is off to the races.

This event happens worldwide, millions of times a year. The estimate of 125 million cats in America is at least equalled in China and gives the reader a sense of cat productivity and proclivity.

A queen will continue to cycle until mated, which leads to an almost-guaranteed litter of kittens sixty-three days later. This period of gestation is as regular as the sun rising daily in the east.

A typical newborn kitten has a slightly disproportioned, dome head compared to the rest of its body. Its eyes and ear canals are closed and miraculously do not open until about day twelve. God's little plan here is so predictable. These events seem to coincide with the emergence from the "ugly duckling" stage to that of a cute, crawling fuzzball. The kitten's eyes, or corneas, have a grayish tint, and their exposure to light must be out of focus, much like that of a human infant. They have a distinct ability to touch and feel, as there is never an inability to find the faucet to nurse. The queen typically has six nursing stations, though some cats have eight. The pecking order is usually a preference of one nipple to each kitten. By the day of eye opening, there will only be the number of functioning mammary glands as the number of kittens in the litter. The let-down of milk is controlled by the oxytocin hormone, which is released by the brain. This physiologic phenomenon crosses all animal life forms. It can best be released by touch and the warm nibbling of the baby. Kittens across all Felidae will use their little front paws in a pulsating, stroking manner as they alternate their pushing and withdrawing motion on their mother's breast like rowing a boat or a grandfather clock pendulum. Once reaching satiation and a full tummy, it seems to strike an accord with the tryptophan factor and a dozing off occurs. At times, they will appear asleep with the nipple in their mouth, only to be jarred back momentarily just to take a few more sucking motions of momma's milk.

The sucking motion for all Mammalia will cause the alimentary tract to spring into action. The rhythm of the nourishment descending through the stomach is not visible but is no less remarkable. This may seem like the gross part, or at least not the most pleasant to the naive observer. A full stomach and the movement of the suckled milk stimulates the gastrointestinal reflex and the need to have a bowel movement. This wiggling dependent relies on the mother to pass this stool and urinate. That same mother's tongue that stimulates the newborn's life at delivery is put into action many times each day.

By three weeks, these bundles of fuzz can crawl and recognize objects. There is no softer or more velvety coat to cuddle than that of a baby kitten. They can be held and petted and only need an occasional reprieve to eat.

Fireball

Ode to Fireball

Fireball was evil, though he had no horns.
Was born on a farm, under a shed of corn.
Church friends found him for Elizabeth and Rick.
Darned cat would bite them, just for a kick.

They could not drive, so pulled in a wagon.
He wasn't too happy and spit like a dragon.
Went each year to visit the vet.
Ornery there too, used a towel for a net.

Big Dr. Al was the puppy's pal.
Met Fireball with the technician gal.
Held on for dear life, 'twas a wrestling event.
A shot in the rump, oh! the anal gland scent.

They gave the guy up, no cats were allowed.
To their buddy the vet, Fireball was endowed.
Find him a home, they confidently said!
Remained a rascal, until he was fed.

To an elderly grandma, Fireball was pawned.
Like toast and jelly, these two would bond.
Scared off the mailman, with his claws through the slot.
Had to baffle the slit, so the letters could drop.

"Free Kittens"—the sign reads. The responsible action by the domestic cat owner is to have the cat altered or spayed before they ever conceive. "Oh, I just want her to have one litter of kittens—then we will have her spayed." This excuse suggests the queen as the one benefiting from the kittens. Nope! They are for the human's enjoyment. The routine scenario is to have a litter and—only being able to find homes for half of them—end up keeping the others for the family. Many multiple cat households fall into this category.

Fireball was born under a corncrib on a country farm in rural Iowa. He was one of four born in the spring at the dawn of the twenty-first century. His mother, Sandy, a svelte, thin queen, lived on a farm with over a dozen other barn cats. It was not unusual to have up to five new litters of kittens on this farm every spring.

Meals for a good mouser or bird nest raider sometimes include leftovers from the family dinner table, and sometimes are supplemented with cows' milk by the farmer. Milk after the butterfat has been removed by the cream separator, though still a healthy supplement, does not provide any fat calories to these often-famished farm cats. In addition, many cats are cow lactose intolerant and have very runny, liquid stools as a result. Attrition on a farm, and tens of thousands like them across America, is a tragedy of cat overpopulation with no practical way of regulating reproduction in the feral population.

Attrition. Just what does that mean? A kitten becomes a cat very early—even as young as four months of age. In order to preserve her own health and regain stamina and weight, the queen, after nursing, will wean the kittens. The kittens have to depend on humans and their own hunting instincts. While nursing, the mother cat will share some of her prey, like a bunny, bird, or rodent, so they will have a knowledge and taste of these creatures. The survival of the fittest can never be understated as the obstacles for such kittens will include parasites, viruses, starvation, murder by marauding tomcats, automobiles, heat and cold, dogs, and animal shelters.

Murder by a tomcat. How can that be? There is a "call of the wild" nature about a territorial, marauding tom. It can be hormonal, seasonal, instinct, or just nature's population control, but the killing of kittens by a tomcat is common. Finding the decapitated body of a young cat or kitten can only lead directly to the villain.

Sandy's foursome litter was reduced in half by a combative tomcat. Fireball was just six weeks old when he was adopted by a handicapped couple. Ricky had a partial clubfoot and a resulting different gait, which caused him to place one foot at a forty-five-degree angle to the ground. His bright red hair matched his ire, at times, and his temper was controlled by medication. His sincere love of kittens was equaled by his kindness to his wife, Elizabeth. Her speech difficulty, due to an apparent mouth problem, made her words come out garbled. She wore print dresses secured by a narrow belt at the waist. Her hair was always neat and secured with a narrow headband. The couple were given the kitten by a church friend. They named this orange and white tabby kitten Fireball, because he was curious and rambunctious. He resisted cuddles from the start. As Fireball grew older, he would bite when being overly petted, and was ornery to Ricky and Elizabeth.

"Do not bite the hand that feeds you." Whoever first spoke those words had never met Fireball. Though he never coddled to being snuggled or caressed, he tolerated sitting on a warm lap for a short while. After being petted for a few minutes, Fireball would lift his head. Looking straight at Ricky's and Elizabeth's faces, showing an evil, hateful expression, he would, for no reason at all, spring to his feet and viciously bite Elizabeth's hand before darting off toward the door like a possessed demon. He would stop there to assess the damage, his blood curdling meow an expression of fright and angst. He would leave the room and not return for several hours. Why? What comes over the nervous system's electronic pathway to trigger this behavior? This devilish, evil expression is one of the standard descriptions other cat owners describe when reporting this action to me, the veterinarian.

※ ※ ※ ※

Fireball came to see me at the veterinary office for his regular checkups and vaccinations. Knowing the couple and Fireball was on the books to come for a visit allowed Cali, the receptionist, to watch out the bay window for their arrival. Arriving in a wagon with a plastic milk crate, Fireball trapped inside, the staff would clear the way for the challenge ahead. Jostling over the sidewalk, the railroad tracks, and every bump in the driveway made this journey a hair-raiser for a disgruntled Fireball. Every second from when Fireball came through the front door to the clinic, until he left following the veterinary examination and procedure, was filled with his evil, blood curdling yowl.

Being the older, more experienced veterinarian, I was always the one scheduled for this task. My veterinarian technician and I prided ourselves on handling difficult cats. Gloved up with combat, elbow length, leather gloves, we opened the bungee-cord-tightened carrier, fished Fireball through the open milk crate, and secured his weapons (his frightful claws) with a heavy towel. Once pinned by Janie's half nelson, Fireball could relax, and vaccinations and a cursory examination were performed. Listening to the heart and lungs while interrupted by growling was rather a joke-for-show by the veterinarian.

One year, a relief veterinarian, Dr. Al Eliason, was seeing patients when dear old Fireball came in for his annuals. Dr. Al was a large, older man with a big barrel chest, arms like tree trunks, and fingers like branches. He had been a large animal practitioner during his active veterinary years. His persona was that he had seen nearly everything and could handle any challenge presented to him.

Then he met Fireball.

Dr. Al was welcomed into the examination room to meet Fireball and his owners. After introducing himself to Ricky and Elizabeth, the good doctor peeked under the blanket, which was hiding the milk crate with an evil cat peering back at him. He had been forewarned of Fireball's antics and personality.

Dr. Al cajoled, "Nice kitty, you don't have to hiss at Dr. Al."

Fireball leered back. *Nice kitty, hell! Don't even try to stick me with a needle, old man!*

Ricky always enjoyed the action of his Fireball getting the best of the poor 'ole veterinarian. He was chuckling and snickering deviously as the circus commenced. It proved to be the price of admission for a ten-round bout. Wrestling a towel over this growling, teeth exposed, claws-flying demon made the grounds slightly more even.

"Now, Miss Becky is going to vaccinate good old Fireball while I just hold him still for a minute," Dr. Al formulated the plan. "Okay, hurry Becky, stick him. I've got a grip on him."

A cat in distress uses every defense in its armor. Fireball sprayed urine and his anal gland odor was billowing. Then came the putrid poop, all over the towel, table, and wall. Now, kitty stool in a small, confined area can overwhelm even the toughest warrior's olfactory senses. Janie peeked under the towel and lifted the skin to inject the distemper sera. Somehow, this near straight-jacket

79

hold failed. Fireball's front leg emerged and snagged Dr. Al's Timex watch band, pulling it about a foot away from the wrist with a claw stuck in one of the links. A calm but perspiring Al did not let this maneuver shake him. He only responded, "Now that's not nice, Fireball—we're just trying to help you!"

Fireball's thoughts were not very complementary. *Old man, next time you try to touch me, you'll be shredded and that watch of yours won't be ticking any longer!* Dr. Al assured Fireball that there was no harm done, and he was sorry he had to hold him with a wrestling grip.

Thank goodness, Fireball's visits to our clinic were limited to his annual exams and vaccination boosters. Had he ever needed medical care, Katy bar the door because an anesthetic to calm him would be the only way to slow him down.

On a picture-perfect autumn morning, I had just unlocked the front door to the clinic. Through the front windows of the reception area, I was shaken by a sight. It was going to be one of those days. Ricky and Elizabeth came, pulling the red wagon with the bungee cords securing the milk crate. It was a scene from a circus parade with the tigers pacing from side to side and pawing at the bars. Yes, it was none other than good old Fireball.

I glanced at the appointment book to see that there was no Fireball scheduled today. I was trapped behind the receptionist desk. "Good morning you two. I see you have your friend with you."

Ricky did not even flinch with remorse when he blurted, "Doc, we have to get rid of the cat because we're moving to another apartment that don't allow cats."

"I'm so sorry; that really is a shame." I frowned, wondering how I fit into this picture.

Ricky quickly replied, "Oh, that's okay. We brought him to you because you were the only one whoever liked him. Can we leave him with you? It shouldn't be hard to find a home for him." I thought, *how in the heck did they ever get the impression that I liked this mean monster?* I must have been a better actor than I thought I was.

And so it was that Fireball, the cat from hell, took up residency at our veterinary clinic. There had been no suggestion of euthanasia, just the kind words, "We know you are the only one who ever liked him!" What an albatross I had inherited.

In biblical terms, "And so it came to pass." Now, I cannot remember ever saying a prayer to the cause, but once again, Gene the office maintenance man and kennel attendant came to the rescue.

Gene was the kindest and gentlest man, who never met a dog or a cat that he did not like. He saw Fireball's cage card with the red sticker that said, "Beware of Cat." I had even taken a marker and emphasized the words with three big exclamation marks behind the sticker. Gene took one look and said, "What's this all about? Fireball is not a nice cat?" Within two days, Fireball was rubbing up against the cage door, waiting to be fed when he heard Gene's voice..

"Gene, do you know of anyone who could use a good orange and white cat?" I asked.

"Well, I guess I could ask Mother. You know her Michael just recently passed away," he mused with sympathy.

By this time, I was really praying that Ruby, Gene's mother, would bail me out.

The adoption, or time out on good behavior, took place. Ruby and Fireball chatted to each other and instantly became great friends. I crossed my fingers that this match would be permanent, and I only got a few reports back indicating that Fireball still had a mean streak in him.

Once, a note was placed through the mail slot in Ruby's front door. The note said that no more mail would be delivered to the residence starting Friday, because every time the mailman tried to deliver the mail through the slot, a mean cat would attack his hands and scratch him. Ruby alerted her son. Once again, it was Gene to the rescue. He built a baffle to extend over the brass mail flap to prevent Fireball from terrorizing the mailman. Through rain, sleet, or snow, the mail was delivered to Ruby and her guard cat, Fireball, the cat from hell.

Mia, My Dear

Ode to Mia

A soccer superstar, Mia Hamm by name,
earned the honor, of a cat by the same.
Mia this little gray and white miss,
had many talents, too numerous to list.

Was found by a roadside, a litter of six.
Rescued by a friend, all covered with ticks.
To a household of cats and even more kids.
Had to find homes for the kitten and sibs.

Megan, her heart set on one under the bed,
'Cuz this little one, 'twas the sweetest, they said.
Proved to be true, only grew to six pounds.
Held her own, however, with Lottie, the hound.

With marbles in mouth, to the stairs to drop.
Releasing them downward, on each step they plopped.
Scampering to the bottom the agate to catch.
Back to the top, she repeated the match.

From the closet, a slipper carried in teeth.
Fetching the mate, placed in hallway very neat.
Guarded them proudly, 'til the owner could get.
Each morning found them, only the edges were wet.

erived from Italian, Spanish, and Slavic backgrounds, Mia means *my, mine,* and *dear darling,* among other interpretations. This dear little Mia blessed the Irish McGillicuddy family. "Mommy, Annmarie from my class at Prairie found some kittens. She must find homes for them. They already have five cats. Her dad had a fit when she and her mother rescued these six kittens from a farm. You said we could have another cat after Bill died. She is saving a kitten for me if you could just take me to her house after my soccer game?" begged eight-year-old Megan. "I don't want them to all be gone, because Annmarie says they are going like hot cakes! What does that mean?"

"Honey, poor old Bill was so sickly. I was just waiting for another opportunity to find another cat for us," Megan's mother confided. "Let's see how soccer goes this morning. Do you know where Annmarie lives?"

In the fall and spring, one can find all the athletic fields scheduled almost every hour of the day with youth soccer on Saturdays in Overland Park, Kansas. Megan with her freckled face, ran the field with authority, her blond pigtails flying. On this day she was a scoring machine, kicking in four goals for a lopsided victory. The final seconds on the game clock ticked off. She darted from midfield to lineup for the high fives and "good game, good game—good game" with the opposing team.

Still with her flushed cheeks and sweat-beaded nose, she rushed to her parents on the sidelines. Brushing off the grass-stained jersey, number 22, and oblivious to the "great game" greetings of other parents, she said, "Mom, you said that if we had time after the game, we could go to Annmarie's to see the kittens. Can we go please? Pretty please?"

The Piepenbring family lived only a few blocks away from the soccer complex. To say they were prolific was an understatement, as seven children under the age of fourteen lived in their two-story, six-bedroom home. Megan's family arrived at lunchtime, adding to the chaos of a house filled with the family, neighborhood kids, and cats.

Unflappable Mrs. Piepenbring met the McGillicuddys at the door apologizing, "Oh, come on in—you'll have to excuse the mess, but it's been a little crazy here this morning."

A little crazy may have been an understatement.

"Annmarie said you would be coming this morning to take one of the new kittens. Annmarie!" Mrs. Piepenbring called, "Your friend is here. Can you show her to the kittens?"

Megan's father Mitchell, slowly tuning in to the message, quipped, "It sounds like this deal has already been made. I should have known."

They were guided to Annmarie's bedroom where kittens were scurrying over the chairs, scattered clothes, and toys on the floor. Megan spotted an active, all-white kitten with one blue eye and one yellow eye. It had gone under the bunk bed and refused to be coaxed out. Finally, Annmarie handed Megan a little gray and white kitten saying, "This one is the sweetest in the litter."

The adoption was official, and Megan caressed the shaking fur ball as the McGillicuddys thanked Mrs. Piepenbring and Annmarie as they departed. "I'm going to call her Mia," Megan softly said. A tear rolled down the cheek of this tough soccer player. "She reminds me of my idol, Mia Hamm, the great soccer star."

Mia was introduced to the family's rambunctious, attention-deficit border collie, Lottie. This dog had a thing for balls. She chased and batted a floppy rubber ball around the backyard for hours on end by herself, almost as if in a trance. Mia sat passively on a deck chair showing no interest or reaction to the ballgame action. Lottie wanted to play with the kitten and was incorrigible, following her around the house. Mia had a way of ignoring the attention and snubbed every one of Lottie's overtures.

Mia loved running up and down the wooden staircase. The hollow step runners echoed with the sounds of her padded feet. She was infatuated with small toys that rolled. After discovering marbles, they became her toy of choice. She was able to hold a wet marble in her dainty mouth. Picking one up, she carefully pranced up the staircase. Reaching the apex, she turned and dropped the wet marble, then patted it to start the game. The marble descended each stair step as momentum and gravity carried it down. "Plip, plop, plip, plop" sounded on each step and the sound was magnified throughout the house. When the marble hit the bottom throw rug, it stopped rolling, and Mia blitzed to the rescue. With the agate back in place at the top of the stairs, the game was repeated until the kitten was exhausted.

Megan was Mia's favorite person in the family. Two younger brothers were occasionally compelled to tie a string on Mia's tail. No amount of cajoling seemed to deter the boys' teasing, so Mia and Megan would retreat to the bedroom for *girl* talk. Sleeping-in was a great life for Mia. She nestled into Megan's side, and her purring vibrated the covers.

By the time Megan was in junior high, the stereo played continually in her bedroom. Mia found an escape from the noise in the guest bedroom. She would crawl up onto grandmother's wedding ring quilt and loved getting under the covers and crawling to the foot of the bed. On her own, the cat could manage to go between the two pillows at the top of the quilt and nose her way under the covers. The family members learned never to place anything on the guest bed without checking first for a lump under the covers.

Soft bedroom slippers were not safe with Mia in the house. Whether left on the floor or in the closet, Mia fixated on the terrycloth fringe and dragged it to the hallway outside the bedroom. How she sensed the match was a mystery, but she could dig through the closet floor to find the mate and pull it into the hallway also. There she sat in the morning, waiting for the first family member to appear and discover her accomplishment. It always brought the reaction, "You crazy cat!" which seemed to be the praise she needed to repeat the stunt the next day.

With both parents working, and the McGillicuddy children busy with after-school activities, Mia often had to fend for herself. The litterbox was all the way down in the basement, and the door was closed inadvertently at times. Along with continual pestering from Lottie, Mia found her own way of taking care of business. Since the boys left the toilet lid up, Miss Mia waited until there was no one in the bathroom. Even with the light turned off, she was able to sneak in and hop up on the porcelain commode to relieve herself.

Mia was an indoor-outdoor cat. Her yard and garden were full of crickets, earthworms, and chipmunks. She was never a hunter but enjoyed pouncing on skittering bugs on the deck. She was able to climb the wooden fence and head off to the neighbor's swimming pool when she pleased. Whenever Mia was missing, she could be found around the pool sleeping and sunning on a pool lounge chair. Every kid loves to have neighbor friends with a pool. Mia was thankful for the open invitation as well.

Mia had an annual malaise or funk. Each year around Christmastime, she gradually stopped eating and became listless. She laid on her tummy with her front paw neatly tucked below. A glaze in her eyes drew attention to her discomfort.

"Has anyone seen the cat?" Mitchell called to the family. The three kids casually located their backpacks and shoes, and their parents set off to work without finding the cat.

Mia had disappeared.

Mitchell worried all morning and came home at noon just to check on her. He found her laying on the tan Afghan blanket on the leather sofa. He greeted, "There you are Miss Mia. Man, you look just as punk as you did yesterday, and your food has not been touched. I don't really have the time, but we are going to the vet."

At the Roeland Park Veterinary Center, Mia was examined. She had no fever and all of her vitals were normal. There was a slight thickening in her lower intestine and a slight pain response when the vet's fingers manipulated her abdomen. Since Mia had shown no signs of vomiting, she was given a small wedge of Pepto-Bismol tablet orally and sent home for observation. Over the next week her attitude, malaise, and anorexia continued. Christmas Day came and went. After New Year's, she made another trip for a recheck at the veterinary clinic. Still perplexed with the baffling syndrome, the vet placed the mercury tipped thermometer into Mia's anal opening. She winced as if to say, *There, do you feel that?* And sure enough, the doctor did sense a gravelly, grating sensation through the insertion of the thermometer tip.

Dr. Freeman said, "Hm, I think she has something in her rectum and colon, a blockage of some sort." With a carefully lubricated forceps, he explored the possible obstruction. Clamping onto a firm mass, he wiggled it back and forth until he expelled it out the bottom anal opening.

"What the heck is that?" an incredulous Mitchell wondered. All encased in a mucous plug was an impaction of pine needles from the Christmas tree. The mystery illness was solved.

Mia returned home to a worried family. She rushed by the welcoming committee and went straight to the food bowl. Even Lottie the collie was shocked to see his cat return home in a much better mood.

Much like a sore muscle, once it is healed and the pain goes away, the incident is forgotten. The following December around Christmas time, the same sickness came upon Mia. Another trip was made to the vet to purge the irritating Scotch pine needles. Mitchell needed the family to vow that next year, an artificial tree would be purchased for the family room.

For the next eighteen Christmases, dear little Mia was able to lay under an artificial tree on a pretty, satin tree skirt and watch in a mesmerizing trance, the twinkling bulbs overhead.

Michael

Ode to Michael

Michael rowed his boat ashore.
Rescued a cat, took him home is the lore.
Was he lost or just a roamer?
Took out ads to find his owner.

Not finding his origin, Michael became his name.
Bringing home prey became the seasonal game.
Bunnies, squirrels, snakes, and frogs,
So proud of his hunting in the woods and bogs.

When the lady at home became terminally ill,
Saved from death row, almost over the hill.
Ruby, a widow lady, rescued this gray.
Each morning on her pillow, he would leisurely lay.

With his outdoor hunting days over for good.
'Twas fed well by the lady, ate all that he could.
His weight skyrocketed, left little to ponder.
Till he joined the two ladies in heaven up yonder.

Michael, row your boat ashore. Hallelujah . . .
Michael, row your boat ashore. Hallelujah!

This ballad was sung around campfires and played on radios throughout the country in the 1960s. The harmonious trio of Peter, Paul, and Mary soothed Americans and the hippie generation during a time when a war divided our nation. During this time, Michael "Mike" Cerone met Connie, a cute little brunette, on a youth hayride. Around a campfire they cuddled and snuggled, wrapped in a blanket. The s'mores, firelight, and crackling of logs emitting sparks into the autumn darkness brought them together. A passionate eighteen-month romance ensued, and they married shortly after graduating from high school.

Mike landed a job immediately with the large John Deere manufacturer in Waterloo, Iowa. Chipping and grinding at the foundry was an entry-level position for many boys who earned their stripes and moved up the ladder. After demonstrating his work ethic, dependability, punctuality, and leadership capabilities, Mike became a supervisor in the tractor assembly plant.

Mike and Connie soon were able to purchase their first home in an area on Cottage Row along the Cedar River. Every afternoon after work and on weekends, Mike would spend hours fishing and boating in the river. The Cedar was backed up by a dam above the falls, and the water roared through the gate to the rocky ledges below. The backed-up water provided a wide, lazy, slow-moving lake above the dam. Walleye, bass, pike, and channel cat flourished in the deep, clean waters.

While fishing and trolling in the backwaters of Snag Creek, Mike spotted a gray cat laying on a log on the shoreline. The cat sprawled and watched him pensively, head rotating slowly as it stared at the passing boat with its trolling motor creeping through the still waters. The cat appeared healthy and well fed. It apparently had a home at one time.

Three evenings in a row, when the boat was floating in the same backwaters, the gray cat was seen in this remote, wooded area. Mike eyed a stump on the shoreline and tossed the front tow line

91

around a fresh beaver-cut stump and beached his flat-bottomed aluminum craft. The gray cat watched the maneuvering and sat up on his haunches, surveying the landing.

"Here kitty-kitty. Here kitty-kitty. It's okay. Can you come here?" Mike pleaded in his soft, kind voice. Swishing its tail and stretching as if doing a pushup with his backend in the air, the cat inched forward to the end of the log. Mike reached out with his hand and the cat pushed his head upward with each stroke. He then allowed long strokes along the torso and back, arching his backend, tail extending skyward like a flag on its mast.

Mike spoke softly to the stray. "Well, old gray guy, I can't just leave you here in this swampy area. How about you come with me, and we'll see if I can find your home."

The cat was tame and climbed onto the man's patched Levi's. Mike balanced and tiptoed along the log and eased back into the flatboat with the cat in his arms. The big gray did not flinch as the trolling motor started with a put-put-put and the boat headed back downstream to the main channel. The pink sunset reflected on the ripples, and the night shadows spread across the water.

Mike cut the motor and docked the boat near the boat ramp. The gray kitty was deposited in the front seat of Mike's blue Ford pickup. As he towed the boat home, Mike was excited to show Connie the latest catch. The gray kitty acted like a co-pilot, watching out the side window while standing with his front paws on the armrest. This cat had obviously traveled in a car before. It showed no fear and made no noise. The Ford's taillights blinked off once they got to the garage, and Mike gathered the cat in his arms.

"Connie, you will not believe what I've brought home," called Mike as he came through the screen door on the back porch.

"Oh! My Lord! Where did you get this gorgeous cat?" cried Connie. She stood in the kitchen, wrapped in an apron and preparing their supper.

Mike had told her about the unfortunate stray, gray cat he had seen on the lake, and she knew this had to be the one. He had not told her that it had lemon-drop yellow eyes and a long tail with dark gray rings all the way to the tip. He recited the story of the rescue mission and the truck ride home and how calm the cat had been.

Gray Kitty walked through the kitchen with ease and looked up to the counters as he sauntered around the butcher block table.

"He must belong to someone. He is so tame and acts so comfortable with being indoors. He must be starving." Connie clasped her hands together, smiling at the beauty of this ring-tailed cat in her kitchen.

Gray Kitty chowed down on breaded catfish and looked up for more. He licked the sides of his mouth politely and methodically with his pointed pink tongue. He carefully licked his paws and commenced to wash his face. Sitting on his haunches, he watched the Cerones eat their supper too.

"Mike, we've got to go to the neighbors to see if they are missing a cat. I'll make some signs to put on the trees and light posts around the school," Connie offered as she planned to search for the true owners.

The Cerones called the humane society inquiring if anyone had reported a missing cat. They knocked on doors the next evening until well after dark. Connie's signs on the poles brought no new "bounty hunters" or leads for this lost cat. She had started calling him Michael after the boat that Michael rowed ashore to rescue him. The leaves had turned colors and fallen from the trees by November. Michael became part of the family. He was a keeper.

Michael was a night owl. He loved all four seasons and would cry to go outside. Much like Tenggren's *Tawny Scrawny Lion*, his prey changed with the seasons. During the summer he dragged home frogs. In the fall he enjoyed catching squirrels. Wintertime served up voles. And in spring a plethora of bunnies would be dropped on the back steps of the house. Michael haunted the woods and riverbanks along Cedar and Snag Creeks. Whether staring down a rabbit or squirrel, the cat's radar inched him forward in the crab-crawl position until a leap midair got him any varmint or moving insect. Cricket and grasshopper populations in the yard dwindled.

On Michael's first visit to Cedar Valley Veterinary Center, I met him in the examination room. "Connie, where in the heck did you find this cat?" I asked while caressing and petting Michael on this first visit. "His back is so long, and this ring tail is so distinctive."

Michael flirted. With his tail held high, he checked out the examination room. He was not frightened by the shiny, stainless-steel examination table or the technician who took his rectal temperature. He may have thought, *Whoa, what are you looking for back there?* as the mercury shaft was pulled out of his back end.

"Your husband rescued him and brought him home? Connie, I don't know if I have seen you after Fluffy died. This cat is so lucky he found you!" I said.

93

Connie brought Michael to the vet every May, like clockwork, for his annual physical examination. No fleas, no heartworm, no ticks, and he was clean of all parasites, as well. I had known Connie for a decade and so enjoyed these annual visits. Hearing of Michael's antics and the way he would drag home his prey added to the enjoyment of the examination. Snakes! Chipmunks! Even fish carcasses from the river showed up on the back steps of the family home.

During one visit, Connie shared that she had breast cancer and that she was worried about her husband's condition. This cat was her confidante and always her soulmate as she struggled through the chemotherapy.

"I'm so touched by your relationship with Michael, and I will include you in my prayers, Connie," I solemnly shared.

The visits to the vet with an aging Michael became more frequent. Little concerns of acne, an ear infection, bad breath, and pawing at the mouth brought Michael and Connie for additional visits.

One morning I reviewed the day's schedule and noted that Connie Cerones was down for an appointment at 10:00AM. The only words behind the appointment were "Michael— EUTHANASIA." I questioned Cali, the head receptionist.

Cali shrugged and said, "The only thing she said was that she wanted Michael put to sleep. She was crying as she hung up the phone."

At 10:00 that morning, I opened the door to the first examination room to find Connie, her face puffy. "Good morning young friend. Can you share with me what is going on here?" I was always cautious about asking why an animal was to be put down, but this was such an unusual request coming from Connie.

It may have been because she had already cried herself to the sense of numbness or that this was just Michael's time. She looked at me with such sad eyes and opened her heart, "Doctor, I have been so blessed to have Michael for the last ten years. You may remember my struggle with the breast cancer and the surgeries last year. He did not leave my side through all the chemo and recoveries. Well, it has come back and has metastasized to my spine. I have been given weeks to live. There is nothing they can do," she said matter-of-factly. "I just don't want him to see me in this pain, and I will not be able to be at home with him. I want him to remember all the happy times and he just can't live without me," she finished.

94

What could a caregiver say in rebuttal? Connie had already signed Michael's death sentence consent form. She wanted me to take the body and did not want any ashes back. I picked him up and hugged Connie with Michael squeezed between us. Both of us had tears trickling down our cheeks. "Connie, God bless you. I know Michael loves you, and I do, too." They were the only clumsy words of assurance that I could muster.

Michael was taken to the cat ward and placed in a cage with a litter pan. In my thirty-five years of loving, counseling, and caring for every animal, great and small, I could not find the courage or the moral ethics to put this perfectly healthy, gorgeous cat to sleep. All the remainder of the day I had visions of Michael rubbing against the front of the cage, turning around, and then rubbing the other side as he meowed to be released from his captivity. That night, after all the office appointments were finished and the paperwork completed, I remembered that I still had Michael waiting to meet the executioner.

I could not do it and decided to go home to see if I could find another plan. I looked in on Michael before leaving for the night. He stretched after his slumber on the sheepskin mat and seemed to say, *I need to tell you, I have no idea why my owner was crying when she left me here today.*

The next morning, I came to the office early before all the staff arrived. There, petting and talking to this big gray Michael, was Gene, the head maintenance and kennel attendant. "What's the deal with this one?" Gene asked. "It says on the cage card euthanasia. He sure looks like a perfectly good cat to me. You're not going to sleep him, are you?"

"Gene, I have an ethical and moral dilemma. The owner brought this cat in to be put to sleep. She has terminal cancer and doesn't want him to be left alone. He is such a good cat, and I just couldn't bring myself to give him the juice yesterday," I explained.

"Well, what do you think if I would check with my mother to see if she would be interested in him? Ever since dad died, she has talked about being lonely and maybe she would be interested in a pet," Gene suggested.

"Oh, Gene! Man, that would be perfect. It sure would relieve my conscience if he could be placed in a perfect home. With no other animals to compete with, he would be such good company for your mom." I smiled and sighed at the possibility.

By mid-morning, Michael was bailed out and no questions were asked. Michael went to live with the ninety-year-old widow, Ruby Walmsley. They hit it off like butter to bread. Seeing her at church the next week, I inquired about her new friend. Ruby, in her Sunday suit and hat with the netting on the front, had a cute smile broadening her face. She said, "So you have heard about my new Michael. He is such a character. I wake each morning and he is sitting by my pillow. He tilts his head at me, wondering if I am ever going to get up and feed him."

Ruby was so happy. All my sins were washed away.

Michael's annual May examinations continued every year. I could see the appointment on the books and paid close attention to watch for Ruby's long, cream-colored Cadillac as it negotiated the turn into the parking lot. She always dressed formally: every day was worth her Sunday best. I always tried to run out to the parking lot to help with Michael's pet carrier. In her inch-high heels, clutching her pocketbook, Ruby followed me up the steps. Into the office and examination room, I lugged the wobbling, heavy pet taxi. I would place the taxi on the table and unlatch the door. Out would walk Mr. Michael, and it was obvious that he had become a couch-potato. He was no longer going outside for his hunting and physical activity regimen. His main duty was caring for Grandma Walmsley.

Logging the history into the records, I always said with a wink, "Well, it looks like Michael has had a very good year. He has only gained one pound." Ruby seemed to think this was a compliment for her great care.

I am not certain if Grandma Walmsley fully caught on that I was hinting that Michael was becoming a bit rotund. But, what the heck, now marking each year of her life into her nineties, it did not make any sense to shame her about Michael becoming obese, though with each extra pound he put on his life was likely shortening. Over the next four years, it was like clockwork. I called him a pound-a-year cat. I had been seeing him for seventeen years, and he had been the stray before that. Living to nearly twenty years was pretty old for a cat. Michael lived a wonderful life until his boat crossed over the River Jordan, with Michael aboard and two wonderful ladies waiting to join him on the other side.

Mr. Tufts

Ode to
Mr. Tufts

He was just a kitten from the forest floor.
This ebon one sent to a pet store.
Bathed and cleaned was ready for sale.
'Tis the start of a wonderful tale.

To a home in the woods, this lucky one came.
Four feline sisters were never the same.
With climbing skills, to heights way above.
There meditated daily, while watching the doves.

While helping the man, through the kitchen pane.
Fell head first, snow below was his bane.
Over his body in the white fluffy stuff.
Shook it off quickly and said that's enough.

The sisters quarreled and even did fight.
He came to the rescue before they could bite.
This debonair guy always over the fray.
Slowed down by age, round the house he lay.

This black silky body, with tufts in his ears.
Succumbed to big "C", after all his years.
But kept for another, his tissues were saved.
Cloning preserved him, reincarnation was made.

Pet stores, like zoos, attract a special crowd of animal lovers. But a zoo is a place where the animals can be seen and not touched. A pet store is where they can be purchased and taken home by an impulse buyer.

A striking, ebon kitten flirted and rubbed its face along the glass window. It paraded back and forth, first one side and then the next. The printed sign said the kitten had been found on a forest trail and was now for sale at Emporium Pet Store. It was nearly three months old with coal black tufts of hair at the tips of its ears and golden yellow eyes. The kitten had an unusually bushy tail and hair between the toes and foot pads. A small patch of white hair resembling a locket perfectly accented a spot at the thoracic inlet.

Tufted hair on the tips of the ear is attractive and makes a cat appear more loveable. These tufts can be particularly useful in preventing dirt and debris from entering the ear canal. They are referred to as lynx tips. The Siberian tufts breed is a cat with these ear tufts and hair between the paw pads, and it is found in the forests of Russia.

When Julianna spotted the kitten, she could not resist. For forty dollars, she bailed the kitten out of the pet store. She brought him to her own home in the wooded area along a ridge above the Cedar River. Upon checking, she knew it was a male. She had four other felines, all female, living in her three-story, rustic A-frame. When the coal black kitten arrived, hissing and batting from the four mean sister-cats ensued.

The new kitten had to have a name. Julianna's husband, Alexander, suggested Mr. Tufts, and the name stuck.

Mr. Tufts made his first visit to see me at the veterinary clinic. When I entered the examination room, I was greeted by an excited Julianna. She said, "Just wait till I show you my new kitty, Doctor!" She reached her hand down the front of her open-necked, flannel shirt and pulled out her new kitten. She always loved seeing me embarrassed, and my face turned red as she produced the cat. Out strode Mr. T with a perfect sense of being and showing no fear.

My eyes and face showed all my appreciation for this incredible looking cat. "Oh Julie, he is beautiful. His long body and that bushy tail with a hook at the end. And the tufts on the ears! And this little tuft of white here on his chest, it looks just like a locket. He looks so much like the European hunter cats with the ear tufts, and those feet have the same characteristics. Wherever did you get him?" I asked.

"He was just a stray found in the forest and brought to the pet store to clean up and sell," Julianna proudly exclaimed.

I got to see Mr. Tufts every other year as he came in for his biennial rabies booster vaccination. It was obvious he was a favorite in the household of five cats. Getting to share in a cat's life with an adoring owner was one of my greatest pleasures as a veterinarian.

Mr. Tufts loved heights. He was an incredible leaper and could walk along the banister and railings to reach the sill above the slider to lay in the sun on the beam above the deck. Like Julie, he showed a dancer's ability of precision and grace. He would sprawl on this ledge of the tall, polygonal window. The view was his first encounter with deer, squirrels, raccoons, and hundreds of birds. With his full bush tail swinging, he nattered away the hours and stared at grosbeaks, downy woodpeckers, and goldfinches. In this home, the four nasty sister-cats could only watch him and wonder if they could ever achieve such beauty. (The sisters did not quite reach the level of Cinderella's ugly stepsisters, but their looks were quite inferior to Mr. Tufts.)

The handsome cat would watch as the nuthatches climbed headfirst down the trunks as they pecked away at invisible nuggets of matter. His ability to concentrate in this position for hours gave him reprieve from the quartet below. When he had enough meditation, he would stand, stretch his sleek torso with the front legs in a crouch, and retreat to the mantel, the bookcase, and then he would jump back down to the floor.

The sister-cats quarreled as a daily pastime. Their snarling and growling at one another eventually led to the sounds of outright warfare. Mr. Tufts' naps were often interrupted as he heard the conflicts brewing from two stories away. He was quite a mediator and would come to the rescue before blood started flowing. His ability to go between the two "mad hens" and disrupt their concentration and disagreement was uncanny.

One day, Mr. Tufts, heeding to the "call of the wild" and noises of nature, ended up at the open kitchen window. Alex had cranked it open and was reaching for the bird feeder with an outstretched arm and a coat hanger. He was trying to resupply the thistle for the goldfinch feeder without going outside in the deep snow. Mr. Tufts sat on the sill and was so fascinated with the operation that he reached out to help. As he stretched, the icicle on the sill edge gave way and down fell poor Mr. Tufts. Cats have perfect righting ability and will always position themselves in a fall to land on their feet. The only problem with this acrobatic feat was that two feet of fresh powdered snow covered the ground. Much like Howard Cosell's rant, "Down goes Frazier, Down goes Frazier!" so went Mr. Tufts.

Alex hurried to the deck walkout door, still wearing his bedroom slippers. Unfazed by the mid-calf depth powdered snow, he shuffled down the steps with a snow rake to the cavernous hole in the massive white drift. "Mr. Tufts, it's me. Can you see the rake? It's right here. There you are, you poor little helper," a panicked Alex yelled.

Scooping the chilled acrobat in his arms, Alex rushed back into the house through the open slider door. Cat and man were covered with the wet clinging snow, and Alex started brushing it away while in front of the fireplace. If cats can laugh at the calamity of a stunt, both Alex and Mr. Tufts were grinning about this escapade. They vowed not to tell Julianna and the four sisters about this windowsill stunt.

*＊ ＊＊

In a multiple cat household, keeping track of five cats and their eating habits and whereabouts can lead to complacency. At bedtime, the roll call always ended with five cats vying for a spot on the king-sized bed in the master bedroom. "They are not all here! It's Mr. Tufts that's missing. He is never late for bed," Julianna pondered. "Alex, wake up," she pleaded as she was prodding her husband. After a half-hour search, the Goldman's posse was called off and both retreated for a restless night's sleep.

Julianna started the search for the lost Mr. Tufts the next morning at the crack of dawn. Upon opening the front door to retrieve the morning *Des Moines Register*, a pitiful meow was heard from under the deck. There he was in his distinct black suit with the white locket on his chest. "Oh, you dear Mr. Tufts! Where have you been and what adventure have you been up to? We have been so worried about you. Your spot was so empty last night in bed. I am sure you are hungry," a joyful Julianna cried. She bent down and Mr. Tufts jumped into her arms.

Mr. Tufts did his head butting and rubbed his whiskered face on both sides of Julianna's face as if to give her the European kiss and greeting. His eyes and face seemed to be saying, *You'll never know what I have seen. The nocturnal life in the woods is anything but quiet. I got carried away when I sauntered out onto the deck last evening. Then somehow the slider got accidently closed behind me.*

The adventure ended well, but it was the last time in Mr. Tufts' seventeen years that he had a chance to do an all-nighter outdoors in the woods.

The mature stepsisters eventually passed on, and Mr. Tufts remained the king of the Goldman household. His daily acrobatic jumps to the perch on the beam above the mantel became more of a challenge. His nightly fits of running the steps and chasing the feathered wand became less an attraction for him. He began sleeping most of the time, curled up in a bed near the hearth. It may have been the arthritis in his legs that made him meow at the bottom of the steps to be carried upstairs at bedtime. He continued to curl in the crook of Julie's leg where his motor-like purring vibrated the covers. When nature caused Julie to get up in the middle of the night, he managed to always jump down to follow her to the bathroom to make sure she was safe.

Mr. Tufts succumbed to an intestinal blockage caused by a constricting multiple myeloma cancer. Julie and Alex brought Mr. Tufts to the clinic for his last visit with a request. "Doctor, I have loved many cats in my lifetime, but there has never been nor will ever be another like Mr. Tufts. Do you believe that he could be cloned? I know this is possible, but I surely want your opinion," she requested.

"Oh, Julie! Let me do some calling and see if this service is possible and, if so, available," I mulled over the idea. I knew that cloning of animals had been done first with Molly the sheep in Scotland. The animal research in mapping the genetic codes of pig, sheep, and cattle had led to such levels that cloning had become possible in these animals. The first pets were reported to have been successfully cloned as well. I made several calls to Cornell University in New York and to another laboratory in Texas. They sent me the protocol and detailed instructions on harvesting the tissues that should be saved, carefully frozen, and preserved for overnight shipping to the Austin laboratory.

Mr. Tufts came to the clinic and seemed to know that this was his last visit to this place where he had been coming for years. With a small mask over his nose, Mr. Tufts relaxed after inhaling the quick-acting anesthetic. A patch was shaved and prepped behind his tufted ear and one on the inside of his groin area. Punch biopsies were taken and carefully placed in sterile vials to be frozen. A staple was placed in the skin where the tissue was removed, and Mr. Tufts was awake again in less than five minutes.

Soon, I was called once again to the little house in the woods to perform the deed that all veterinarians dread. Mr. Tufts was purring when I reached to hold his leg and found the vein. Tears of love and gratefulness of having had such a wonderful friend in their lives were shed over this beautiful and loyal cat.

Julianna received a call from the Texas genetic and research laboratory. Mr. Tufts' cells had been propagated and had been implanted into a surrogate queen. It was a successful match, and they were extremely optimistic that she was pregnant with the cells of Mr. Tufts. The next nine weeks could not go fast enough. The mystery and suspense of waiting was overwhelming. Julianna and Alex had never had such a catless household in their married lives.

A call in December came from the laboratory that a black kitten with a small wisp of white on its chest had been born that morning. Julie and Alex hugged with joy, and the handkerchiefs and tissues were employed.

Science, technology, and engineering had made this cloning possible. On that morning it was just another little kitten born, although it was a test tube baby. For the next eight weeks, the Goldmans face-timed with Amanda, the technician at the cloning laboratory. The kitten was shown to them as it opened its eyes for the first time at nineteen days. He nursed his mother's white breast. His coal black torso moved in rhythm as the little front feet massaged the mammary gland while he suckled. It was like watching the weekly metamorphosis through a window. Amanda was very patient and showed her affection for both the kitten and his surrogate mother, Cinderella. Julianna was so amazed and thankful that she offered to adopt Cinderella if she could be transported safely. The deal was approved and set in motion. At nine weeks old, Mr. Tufts Jr. and Cinderella were flown to Iowa with Amanda, the technician from the Texas laboratory.

The Goldmans set off for the Cedar Rapids airport to meet their new Mr. Tufts. They discussed his name. Since he was genetically identical to Mr. Tufts, why not just call him Mr. Tufts, also. The couple giggled as they waited for the escalator and their incoming treasure. A brunette carrying an almond pet taxi was descending the long moving stairs. Julianna's face was radiant, and her hands were clasped in excitement. Hugging someone you have never met may seem awkward, but this rendezvous was special. Shuffling to a side bench, Amanda beamed and said, "Oh, you wonderful people. I can hardly wait to take off this protective cover to show you your new kitty. He is gorgeous."

As she unzipped the cover and opened the front door of the pet taxi, out walked the coal black kitten. He seemed no worse for wear following the three-hour flight.

Julianna's eyes watered as she watched this remarkable image of her Mr. Tufts before her, strutting down the bench planks. "I cannot believe my eyes. This is a flashback. He is my Mr. Tufts reincarnated. The tufted ears, the pointed face, the long bushy tail with the little kink at the end, and of course the hairy feet and the white locket. This is remarkable. No, incredible! Or maybe just unbelievable!" She gasped with joy, clutching her handkerchief. "And look who else is here. His mother!" Cinderella was more reserved with the bustling travelers rolling their luggage in the hallway around the lounge seating.

Mr. Tufts took the hour-long ride home in Julianna's arms. He loved to snuggle. He closed his eyes in her cradled arms and listened to the clicking of the tires on the pavement and the sound echoing as the SUV made its way home. The kitten slept deeply with rhythmic purring emanating from his restful body.

From Julianna's arms to the bookcase, to the mantel, then to the beam over the slider, Mr. Tufts was once again home in the woods.

Nuisance

Ode to Nuisance

A cat named Nuisance, his image would be.
In the fishing skiff, at the helm you see.
Days on the Cedar, he spent with his buddy,
Leaped to the dock, feet never got muddy.

This orange colored one, loved to fish.
Replaced two dogs, was the angler's wish.
Found under a boat, on a crisp spring morn.
He meowed for help, was sadly forlorn.

Lived in town with this elderly couple,
Climbing a tree, his movements supple.
Stayed out at nights, the neighbors all loved.
Fit through the cat door, like a hand in a glove.

Helped clean the fish, the fillets were bared.
Catfish his favorite, always given his share.
At fisherman's wharf, was known by all.
This man and his cat, pic on the clubhouse wall.

Three men. Childhood buddies. World War II Veterans. Three musketeers. They each lived to nearly ninety-years old. All were grumpy old men with a passion for fishing.

Male companionship and bonding at its best found this trio in their boats with their dogs trying to catch just one more fish for bragging rights. Bob Johnson, Robert Purdy, and Darrel Porter loved nature and the ever-changing outdoors. Each morning, they met in their fishing boats on the Cedar River to cast their lines. As they aged, their shouts to each other echoed across the still waters to Main Street. As hearing impairments progressed, the bantering and cajoling amplified a few decibels.

Each had a dog in the boat that sat at the helm like a trained navigator. The river was like glass, stilled by a dam from the falls below. The current slowly pushed the waters eastward. Fishing was excellent in the early mornings and evenings. The threesome each had their favorite bait and lures as they explored the inlets and streams. Banter included fishing techniques as well as stories about their favorite kind of fish to catch. Darrel was a walleye fanatic. Big Bob swore by the river bass. Bob "Catfish" Johnson was just that, a catfish man. He was also nicknamed "Catfish" after a Kansas City A's (Kansas City Athletics) young, right-handed pitcher named Catfish Hunter.

Bob's faithful boatmate was Nuisance, an inquisitive little beagle. Nus, as he was known to all, became excited when a fish was on the hook. His trademark beagle yowling let everyone know that Bob was pulling them in like the biblical fisherman Andrew. Ole Nus kept the morning air lively with his greetings. Even on a foggy morning, there was no question of where Catfish Bob and Nus were on the river. Above the humming and sputtering of the trolling motor, the other grumpy old men often yelled at Nus for chasing away *their* fish with his baying.

Nuisance was a swimmer and at times became so excited that he would jump overboard. In one leap, he would splash right into the river after a flipping fish on the hook.

Darrel's dog was a stoic black lab named Buck who much preferred more action than fishing and sitting in a boat. Hunting and retrieving were his thing. Fishing was too sedate a sport for him. His erect, statue-like pose on the front seat seldom changed as he searched earnestly for something to retrieve.

Bob Purdy's Matilda was a feisty Jack Russell who was as tough as nails. She hung over the side of the boat looking for fish and even peering at her own reflection in the water. She was ready to do whatever Bob needed.

The three musketeers, three dogs, and three flatboats were fixtures of comradeship until the bond was broken. Old Nus reached old age and went off to chase fish in the sky. Catfish Bob was deeply saddened to lose his great pal of nearly fifteen years. The other men challenged him to get a "real" dog. They were surprised when, one morning, Bob showed up with a new, roly-poly Golden Retriever puppy. However, a problem occurred when the only thing retrieved was the new dog, Sam, when she fell overboard. The annals of dog history do not report of a dog that could not swim, but Sam sank like a two-ton rock, and Bob had to "retrieve her." In fact, she was terrified of the water. Bob tried various, gentle training tricks such as a stick and ball tossed in the shallow water to entice Sam. She refused to get even a foot in the water. Somehow, the synapse and retrieving chromosome failed to kick in. None-the-less, Bob and his new pal were loyal to each other for the next ten years.

Sam would trudge along to the dock. She was lifted into the boat, strapped into a doggie life jacket, and would shiver with angst through the morning float. Catfish withstood the hoots and hollers from his pals as his loyalty to his hydrophobic dog remained.

In the days after "good ole' Sam" was put to rest, Bob told his wife, "Shirley, I just can't go through this again. At my age, I can't have another dog. I am sure it would outlive me, and I get so attached to them. Even Ole' Sam, the scaredy-cat dog, was my best buddy."

Shirley smiled and lovingly said, "That's okay for now to say that, but you said the same thing ten years ago when Nuisance died."

Throughout the winter, Bob had no one to sit beside him in his recliner. When pushed to the screened-in porch to ruminate and suck on his cigar, he had no one to commiserate with about the unfairness of not being allowed to smoke his sweet-smelling cigar in the house. As he tottered along on the frequently slick Iowa winter sidewalks with his cane, there was no one to join him on the fresh crisp morning jaunts around the block.

When the ice began to break up on the river shorelines and the backwaters were opening, Bob drove down to the boathouse to get a glimpse again of the springtime waters of his childhood. The quiet was only punctuated by the honking of the Canadian geese surveying the shorelines. His new hearing aids were tuned into the solitude when a desperate meowing sound under a boat trailer directed him to look under the hitch. Bending down on his arthritic knees, Catfish came eye to eye with a pitiful looking cat.

"Why you, old fella, come over here," he coaxed the scrawny, orange-colored cat. It stretched and inched toward Bob. The cat rubbed his face and whiskers against Catfish's Carhartt jacket. "How can you be purring on this chilly morning? You come with me, and I'll see if I can get you warmed up with some breakfast."

Slowly getting to his feet with the cat in his arms, Bob ambled to the pickup truck. The keys jingled as the motor revved and the heater was cranked to high. The perfect white vest of this orange boy rested on Bob's knee as they headed up the Cottage Row gravel road toward town.

Without going home, Bob stopped at my office on the south side of the Cedar River. "Doc, I've gone and done it again. This old fella seemed to be calling my name. I just had to pick him up. Can you fix him up and whatever you need to do? I think I'll call him Nuisance Two because he is sure going to give me a few runs for my money," Bob said smiling and looking over his bifocals.

I chuckled and assured him that this kitty looked to be less than a year old. "You know, Bob, I think Nuisance Two is a perfect name for him. He's already been neutered, so at least his catting days are behind him. He looks a little wormy but should clean up fine. How about leaving him with me this morning, and we'll bathe him and get him vaccinated and dewormed. He looks like he's starved, so we'll set the table for him."

Bob grinned, and it was a joy to see him so happy. The last time I had seen him was on the frigid Sunday morning in his greenhouse when Sam was put to sleep. My teenage daughter, Carolyn, was helping me, and the tears rolled down both of our cheeks when a consoling Bob held Sam in his arms and said, "Good-bye ole Sam. I'll meet you on the other side."

The grumpy old men met at 7:00 on Friday mornings at the Happy Chef restaurant to discuss the weather and prospects for spring fishing. They always tried to be the first fishermen on the river when the ice had dissipated from the shorelines. Bob held his cards close to his chest and did not tell his friends that he might have a new fishing buddy. He knew the hooting would come soon enough.

St. Patrick's Day came, and the three musketeers met as planned. Their trailers backed up to the water and exhaust vapors from the pickups wafted in the still morning air. The ramp was still slick as each of the boats was eased into the calm morning waters. Steam rose as cool morning air hit the water surface. Matilda and Buck snooped the rocky shoreline exploring the many interesting smells. Luckily, the Evinrude outboard motors started on the first pull, and the gear was all loaded into the hull.

Bob announced, "Hey, will you hold my tow line for a second? I need to go back to my truck to get something." He hobbled up the slick concrete, sloping ramp and fetched his new pal. "I want you to meet my new fishing buddy. This is Nuisance Two. Look—no life jacket on him," Bob exclaimed, an ornery and radiant smile broadening his face.

There are times when special friends recognize the sensitivity of a friend's feelings and refrain from even the gentlest of teasing. Catfish Bob and Nuisance Two boarded their boat and it was "ships ahoy." Nuisance Two took to the water like a Navy first mate. He perched on the cross plate at the helm, showing no fear. His eyes focused on the water and the other boats like a most observant navigator. The first catch of the spring was pulled in by Bob—a three-pound catfish. Nuisance Two watched with intense interest as the fish flopped on the boat's bottom. Bob hooked the fish onto a stringer which was then carefully dropped back over the boat's edge. Nuisance Two watched the fish serpentine under the water.

What a red-letter day they had! Bob was hot, and the fish were biting. In two hours, the stringer was full, and the duo was back in the truck. They headed for home to the gutting table in the backyard fish hut. Nuisance Two hopped up on the table and watched intently as the fillet knife glided like a scythe under the fish's skin. He must have been thinking, *I don't know what all this slimy looking stuff is, but it sure smells like something good to eat.*

"Well, old Nus—how about a piece of catfish?" Bob asked his first mate. He pushed over a square of meat to Nus who was already licking his lips.

"Wow, I guess it was meant to be. It's just you and me now. Who would have ever thought I'd have a cat for my boating mate, and we both like catfish?" Bob grinned at his cat sitting at the end of the butcher block table, washing his face with his paws.

The duo became fixtures along the river. Whenever Bob slept in or a rainy non-fishing day came along, Nuisance was right there to wake him. He rubbed his face along Bob's whiskered cheek. His meowing and body language urged, *Daylight's burnin'. Let's get up and head for the river.*

The other grumpy old men even complimented Bob on his new fishing buddy. The cat was so agile. He could run down the dock and jump three feet to the boat's edge. An accomplished acrobat—he never missed a step. They had to admit that the cat was almost as good as a fishing dog.

Was it just trying to please his human, or was it truly the case? Nuisance Two seemed to prefer catfish over bass or walleye. Though he never refused any aquatic morsel, if given an option, he chose catfish every time.

At home, Bob installed a cat door in the kitchen wall. Nuisance could come and go as he pleased. He was quite an agile tree climber, and the large oak tree in the back yard was his favorite. He crawled to the top, sitting in the "crow's nest" of an imaginary ship to scan the horizon for activity. He only needed a sailor's cap and telescope to complete his image. No amount of coaxing could bring him down from this treetop perch before he was ready. When the lights were all turned off for bedtime, he would back down the tree, and the spring latch on the cat door squeaked as the nighttime prowling came to an end and he headed off to the bunk room.

Successive years of extreme flooding of the Cedar River started in 1993. A very wet rainy fall followed by a bone-chilling winter created heavy ice formations in the river and its tributaries north into southern Minnesota. In March, the rains came. The already saturated frozen soil allowed no rain to be absorbed. Draining of the sloughs and the intense tilling of the farmlands in the previous thirty years made the runoff to the drainage basin increase exponentially. The 1993 flood was considered a five-hundred-year flood. It was followed by even larger high-water depths in 1997. Then the granddaddy of them all swept through the basin in 2008.

It was with one another's support, the old grumpy men decided to hang up their morning boating routine. Too often, families agonize over having to take car keys away from mom or dad to keep them from driving in their advanced years. At the weekly coffee gatherings, the three men were able to discuss their options and admit some of their boyhood talents were behind them.

Darrel shared that his Buck had not made it through the winter. He choked up telling of the talented bird dog and the hours they had spent in duck blinds that were now over. Robert's Matilda had become a diabetic. This caused her to lose her eyesight once the disease made her lenses crystalize like cataracts. They lamented that without their dogs and with the most recent flooding, there was a likelihood that their fishing days were behind them. Catfish Bob avoided thinking that his ever-present use of his cane might limit his access to getting into a boat.

Nuisance Two seemed to sense the change in the air. Catfish Bob was not able to accompany him on twice-daily walks. The boat remained in the garage under a tarp. The cat paraded around the house meowing while looking for some activity. Bob had always hoped that he would outlive his dogs and now his cat.

And then it happened that the weather caused more trouble on the Sunday before Memorial Day. A category-five tornado, just twenty miles west of Bob's place, devastated Parkersburg and the countryside as it progressed east to New Hartford. I received a page from the answering service reporting a dog owned by Diane Sullivan, Jellybean, had been through the 180 mile-per-hour vortex and was in critical shape. I met her at the clinic that evening. The blue heeler was in shock. Her face and entire body were edematous and puffy, suggesting she had been rolled or hit and pelted with gravel. It was not known if she had been lifted into the vortex or if she had been thrown for any distance. I gave her supportive therapy and hospitalized her that night. As I helped Diane back to her car she sadly said, "I am missing my cat as well. I know you'll think I am making this up, but ironically her name is Twister."

Miraculously, Jellybean survived and was able to go home the next night. Diane was thrilled to pick up her dog but reported that there was still no sight of her cat.

Two weeks later, at the peak of the June flood, Catfish Bob came to see me at the office. Placing his cane on the table, he asked for my advice and help. "Doc, I think I need to give up the ship. I still have the heart, but my darned arthritis is getting the best of me. Then, I have my fishing buddy, Nuisance. He still begs to go with me, and I can't do it. It breaks my heart to see him so cooped up inside with me."

I listened to his story and knew he would request that I help him find a new home for Nuisance Two.

Bob continued, "So, Jim, do you know of anyone who could give him a good home and maybe make him happier?"

I immediately thought of Diane, Jellybean, and the lost cat, Twister. "You know Bob, I may just have a happy life ahead for Nuisance. There was a lady who lost her cat in the tornado two weeks ago, and this may be the ticket for your dear friend."

A call to Diane found her pleased to rescue a cat for another new chapter for her family. She drove to town and together we went to Bob's home. Catfish Bob met us with a wry smile and introduced Nuisance to this nice lady.

Nuisance Two crawled onto Diane's lap and the bond was made. He went home that day to live in a country house. He started his next chapter of helping yet another human who was grieving over the loss of a beloved family pet.

Patches

Ode to Patches

Her personality so wonderful, none could compare.
Saved by a vet at the "dairy"iere.
Black, orange, and white in a pattern laid
Exposed tail end, a farm mutt had made.

Calico Patches and sister, fall kittens they were.
Malnourished and dying without even a purr.
Eyes matted and sniffles from nose,
As the vet rescued them, their spirits arose.

Defleaed, deloused, dewormed, and bathed.
Brought from the dead as everyone raved.
Patches the beauty soon won everyone's hearts.
Became the clinic cat, known for her smarts.

Leaping over the counter to meet every dog and cat.
Not frightened by any, just flirted and sat.
Any open carrier or purse found Patches inside.
Made herself comfy, hoping for a ride.

One day asleep in the dryer, wet clothes were thrown in.
Thumpity, thump! when it went for a spin.
Emergency sound, the dryer door opened to surmise.
And out leaped this Houdini cat, 'twas quite a surprise.

A contaminated vaccine, cancer-causing took her life.
Many mourned her, four times under the knife.
A spreading sarcoma mass under the skin.
Killed the dear calico, as it invaded within.

The name Patches needs no explanation. The distinctive orange, black, and white colors of a calico cat are a beautiful sight. Joseph's "coat of many colors" could not have been more striking. Born in a dairy barn in Iowa in 1981, Patches and her sister Misty were aberrations, part of a late fall litter of haystack kittens. Such litters are given little chance of survival in the winter months due to disease, malnutrition, tomcats, and weather. Iowa winters drive farm cats into buildings and barns for warmth. These kittens' mother had tried to nurse them but abandoned them in the dairy barn at six weeks of age.

The coziness and aroma of a dairy barn in the fall was a scene common to thousands of family farms in the twentieth century. Whether Holsteins, Jerseys, Guernseys, or Ayrshires—these docile breeds of cow were kept inside, protected from weather elements of the late fall and long winters of the Upper Midwest. These gentle milk factories can each weigh over a thousand pounds.

For milking, each individual cow is fastened in place by a stanchion or tethering chain. The mangers for food and water spickets are mounted at the front of the cows. Their back ends are adjacent to the gutter, which collects their waste, and a circulating gutter cleanser mechanically removes it to an outside spreader. The combination of the cows, the sweet smell of corn silage, molasses laced grain of oats and corn, crisp dried alfalfa squares, and the white-limed alleys all together emit aromas for an olfactory smorgasbord.

I arrived at this particular dairy for a late afternoon call to examine a cow that was off her feed. Walking into the alley of the barn, I glanced at the straw bales to the side of me to see two little kittens playing. The gorgeous calico caught my eye as I made my way down the center, lime-covered alleyway to examine this huge momma Holstein.

Clyde directed me to the cow, which he had called me for that morning to treat. "What symptoms are you seeing?" I asked.

The bewhiskered, scruffy-bearded farmer lit an unfiltered Camel. He said with empathy, "She's just not herself. Her milk production is dropping every day. I ran a paddle (checking for infection in the udders) and it looks clean." His weary facial expression showed his concern. I was aware of the extreme difficulties with low milk prices, and the impending stress of bills and bank closings on so many farm operations in the 1980s. I took the cow's temperature, listened to the heart and lungs, examined the stomachs (cows have four), checked mammary glands for mastitis, and ran a ketone test on the urine.

"Clyde, this old girl has ketosis," I explained. Ketosis occurs a few weeks after calving in high milk producing dairy cows when their energy intake is not as great as their energy output. The cow starts breaking down body fat which then overloads the liver's ability to breakdown ketones. This causes acetonemia, an elevation of acetones in the blood, resulting in an extremely sick cow. After treating her with an intravenous solution of dextrose, vitamins, and a stimulant dose of corticosteroids, I closed my medicine bag. As I made my way toward the milk house to clean up the IV set, I spotted the kittens rolled up in a ball on a gunny sack. The little calico had a wet tail and opened its eyes as I reached down to pet them. The tip of the tail looked hard and, on closer examination, I noticed that the last two inches of her tail tip had exposed coccygeal vertebrae. "Clyde, have you noticed this kitten being chewed on by anything?" I questioned.

"Oh, yeah," he casually said. "The dog really plays with them, and I've seen him chewing on that one's tail."

I tried not to show my astonishment but asked, "You know these fall kittens are not long for the world. Has their mother abandoned them?"

"Yeah, I think she got stepped on by a cow a few days ago, and I haven't seen her since. What do you think I should do with them?" Clyde asked.

"Well, I think I could find them a home if you would like me to take them with me." I tried to hide my special love of kittens and calicos.

Clyde jumped at the offer, "Sure why don't you take them—they're just going to die here. I got too much going on to try to nurse them along."

I scooped the calico and her sister into my arms. I washed my boots before getting back into my veterinary pickup truck. These little girls were remarkably passive and did not even wiggle as we bounced out of the farm driveway.

The early winter skies were golden. The country road was lined by the tall corn still standing in the field with ears hanging, beckoning for the late harvest. Two sun dogs glowed in the southwest sky as the pumpkin-colored orb dipped below the horizon. The half-hour drive over the potholed gravel roads to the clinic was punctuated by my glances down at the placid little ones nuzzled in the crook of my arm.

Picking up the handset of the two-way radio, I called back to the office, "KNCR 983, this is Unit 1. Come in. Would you get me a hot water bottle ready? I am bringing in a couple of weak, emaciated kittens."

It gets dark early in December, but there were still client cars in the clinic parking lot when I arrived. I entered the back door quietly with my orphaned kittens. Better light and closer examination on the stainless-steel table revealed the most incredible living museum for a parasitologist to envy. There were roundworms, hookworms, tapeworms, ear mites, lice, fleas, and coccidia. Any one of these by itself is enough to put a kitten out of commission. These one-pound infant kittens were struggling against at least seven obvious foreigners.

A careful flea bath, ear mite drops, worming, and sulfa antibiotic were administered. I was already calling the calico Patches. Her tail tip was so hard and dead that when it was snipped off with scissors, she did not make a whimper or show any sign of pain. No bleeding confirmed there was no viability in the tiny coccygeal vertebrae at the tail tip. A topical antibiotic and small tape band aid was secured over the now-shorter tail. I named the other kitten, with her black undercoat and whitish accents, Misty.

Patches and Misty were offered their first nourishment. They quickly inhaled the slurry of milk and kitten gruel put before them. When seeing ravenous kittens try to eat at this young age, the term *inhale* is not too far-fetched. They put both of their front paws and face down into the Fiestaware saucer. If ever there was a time for a bib, this was it. Saturation was soon reached, but not before each of them vocalized an aggressive, growling, protecting-my-food sound as they snarfed down the first real meal they had ever eaten. I was delighted to witness them eating, sneezing bubbles from their nostrils, with whiskers coated with gruel. Both kittens licked their lips and tried to clean their faces with their dainty front paws.

After a warm washcloth to the face and paws, Patches and Misty curled up in a ball together on a pink fluffy towel with a heating pad below.

Parasites and other varmints of all persuasions came out in the litter pan. That a six-week-old kitten knows what to do in a litter pan is as instinctive as nursing, purring, and licking the paws to clean their own faces. Oh, the beauty of a cat of any age methodically licking its paws and wrapping a paw over its head and face to tidy up. No preening of a beautiful lady in front of a full-length mirror could be so pleasant to watch.

In no time at all, these two orphans were ready for a trial run at my own home. There was only one hurdle to overcome—the lady of the house was allergic to cat dander. Her eyes would start to itch and water instantly in a cat's presence. Yet, into our home the kittens came. Our two daughters loved dressing the kittens up in doll clothes and parading them around in a baby stroller. Their personalities and antics of string chasing, batting ping-pong balls across the floor, and catching cotton balls in midair were enjoyed for hours on end.

After several weeks of much love and bonding, the allergies of the lady at home could not be overlooked or ignored. A difficult decision had to be made. I would have to find different homes for the kittens. After a few tears from the family, the kittens were boxed up for the trip back to the veterinary office. Misty went home with the front office receptionist, Cali, but Patches stayed at the clinic and became the official Calico Greeting Cat.

Patches truly greeted every client who entered the door as the bell suspended on a string at the door announced their arrival. Running and jumping upon the counter to be the first to welcome the outsider, Patches assumed that everyone thought she was head of hospitality. Big purses left unattended found her coiled on top of the contents, looking like she was part of the package. Animal carriers with doors left open found Patches hiding inside. What a surprise the owner's cat or dog found when, following the veterinary examination, it was shoved back in its kennel now occupied by the tricolor intruder. Hisses and whining concluded as Patches made a hasty but teasing retreat as she paraded through the open-grated cage door.

When Patches was not in a purse or pet taxi, she comfortably hopped up on the instrument counter to observe as each pet was presented for an ailment or examination. Dogs did not intimidate her in the least. Patches sensed that she owned the place, and most of them were restrained from chasing her by a leash. How frustrated the dogs seemed when this flirtatious feline, who was supposed to run up a tree when pursued, would just lift her tail and rub against the table leg or door jamb just out of the dog's reach. She did meet her match when Skippy, a 200-pound Mortdecai-colored Great Dane jumped over the examination table and leaped for the flirting Patches. She narrowly escaped the savage, snapping teeth of Skippy with his astonished handler holding on to the leash for dear life.

Our veterinary clinic also provided pet grooming. Patches loved to jump up on the grooming table and shock the dogs. With the dogs' heads and necks secured to a safety hook by a soft leash, they were unable to snap and send this bold cat on her way. She knew they could not get her, and she taunted them by walking under their bodies as they stood still for their haircuts. It had to be the crowning insult to their dignity.

The laundry was a frequent site where Patches could be found. She was often at the bottom of a pile of warm towels on the counter, waiting to be folded. This ingenious cat would hide her whole body under the heap of towels with only a wagging tail on the backside of the heap of laundry to give away her hiding place. A dryer door left open meant surely it was a place to curl up and sleep. On a few occasions, the laundry towels were taken from the washer and thrown into the front-loading dryer. It wasn't until the knob turned to start the dryer that a screaming and thumping would be heard. If ever one has heard the thumping of tennis shoes in a washer or dryer, imagine hearing a cat being pounded and thumped as a dryer started with Patches inside. Wow— the panicked laundry attendant, alarmed by this unusual pounding noise, hastily opened the front door of the dryer. Out jumped a disgusted Patches with a look of *How could you be such a klutz to start the dryer with me inside?!* on her face. Sauntering off to greet the clients for the rest of the day was her way of getting past the embarrassing ordeal.

Not many cats visiting the vet come of their own volition. Fractious, mad, and sullen expressions are only a few of the greetings a veterinarian is challenged with when opening a pet taxi with a cat in it. I prided myself on trying not to make this panicked visit any more traumatic than it needed to be. Many tricks and techniques are used to sneak a look or a hand in to restrain the occasional vicious teeth and claws while crooning "nice kitty." Patches was most attracted to a yowling and growling patient. The ornerier, the better for this mistress of the house. Patches would come running from the other end of the clinic or grooming room just to be in on the action. Of course, her help was the last thing the poor sweating vet needed to calm a distraught patient and an owner who thinks "this is not like her Fluffy!"

Patches often came home with me on weekends to take a break from her veterinary hospitality duties. We would let her outside to walk in the grass and smell all of nature's scents. Her only extended stay with our family was on the occasion of her maternity leave.

The expression of "the cobbler's kids wear no shoes" could be applied to this clinic cat and her frequently expired vaccinations. The needle deed was always relegated to me, and I could hardly bear to stick my own beautiful Patches kitty. Now, in vaccinating any animal with a syringe of serum, there are preferred sites for these inoculations. By far the easiest and safest is under the skin in the base of the neck region. Safe because the biting end of the patient can be secured with a headlock or a grasp of the scruff of the neck with the other hand.

In the early '90s, there was a vaccine released for feline leukemia virus. It was a breakthrough vaccine for cats to prevent the deadly communicable disease which eventually kills the feline. There were serum antigen tests available twenty years earlier to detect if a kitten or cat was a carrier of the virus. However, there was no prevention to protect the cat population from the virus until this breakthrough discovery. With any new drug or preventative vaccine, there are warnings and a long insert in the vial with protocol from the manufacturer. The trials, research, and ultimately FDA approval are all assurances that a medication is safe to use.

A new syndrome was being reported in veterinary scientific research journals and at veterinary continuing education conferences. A sarcoma tumor growth had been developing in cats at injection sites of a vaccination. The specific suspicious vaccine or the manufacturer was not defined. We had no idea which product was the culprit. With millions of cats being vaccinated, it should have been determined through epidemiologic methods—the who, why, which, and what was happening.

I will not divulge the company that had the impurity of the cancer-causing virus contaminating their feline leukemia vaccine causing the sarcoma reaction. As a veterinarian, I had taken the oath and based my word on the motto of "do no harm." Our clinic used this new vaccine and had no reactions in hundreds of cats. Was there just one bad batch of vaccine and had it been stopped and caught by the manufacturer's quality control? I sincerely hoped so.

Finally, after nagging by the veterinary staff at the clinic, the three overdue vaccines for Patches—rabies, distemper, and leukemia—were drawn up by the nurse and handed to me. With the dastardly deed completed, I could rest for another year before the requests from my dear staff to vaccinate Patches showed up on posted notes on the laboratory door.

Within two weeks of the shots, a hard lump was noted on Patches' neck. Denial and postulations conjured in my mind. The lump was lobular and started in the exact location of the leukemia inoculation. Could this be the deadly sarcoma being described in the scientific literature?

A surgery was scheduled to do an elliptical incision to remove the invading cancer. With the first surgery on the dorsal cervical neck completed, we could only wait and see if the surgeon was successful in removing this rapidly growing and spreading mass. In only two weeks, the healed incision site was again starting to form small, hard, pea-sized lumps under the surface of the skin.

Three more surgeries over the next five months proved unsuccessful, even with each being more radical in the removal of muscle, subcutaneous tissue, and ever wider margins of the skin. Patches' agility became affected. Her head was so stiff from scar tissue that she could not jump and help with the clinic greeting, or in the examination room. All the clients coming in to see her and the vet were missing her, and they too were crushed by her impending demise.

Though my veterinary office used a few thousand cases of vaccine each year, Patches, our lovely calico, was the only cat ever to show this dreaded cancer virus. It might have been an omen, or at least a weird blessing, that she was the only one affected at my clinic, as other reports from nearly all the local, state, and national veterinarians reported their own stories and mostly fatal results.

A cat is just a cat until it is your own cat. It has been nearly thirty years since this tragic vaccine induced the death of my dear Patches. I can still see her pitiful face and eyes looking up at me, seeming to say, *You have always helped me. Why is this happening to me?*

It still breaks my heart to remember. Cats are all beautiful in someone's eyes, but my Patches really was a darned beautiful cat.

Siamese Cats

The first well-documented history of a Siamese cat in the United States was a gift to First Lady Lucy Webb Hayes, wife of President Rutherford B. Hayes, in 1879. The gift-giver was David B. Sickels who was serving as the American Consul in Siam (modern-day Thailand). The Siamese had already become the cat of socialites in Europe by this time. There are cats resembling the Siamese on the stone carvings in Egyptian temples from over two millennia before.

Across Europe and North America, the Siamese soon became a popular breed for indoor feline aficionados. They are noted for their big ears, dainty triangular shaped heads, almond-shaped blue eyes, and long sleek bodies. The most prominent colors and lines are Seal Point, Chocolate Point, and Blue Point. Other colors and bloodlines that have evolved in the last fifty years are Peach, Lilac, Fawn, Carmel, Cinnamon Red, Tortie, and Tabby.

The *Lady and the Tramp* movie from the 1950s features two Siamese cats, Si and Am, who taunted poor little Lady. They sang in their aristocratic twang about their breed, a pleasing tune that sticks in the memory.

Percy

Ode to Percy

This cat named Percy, a clarinetist's boy,
Many a symphony, they did enjoy.
Lived this Siamese in a bachelor's pad.
Jamming and singing with his professor dad.

Loved the aquarium and the fish he saw.
Touched the gouramis as he dipped in his paw.
One Pete Fountain and Benny Goodman another,
Watched for hours on the heated cover.

Had a thing for water, showers the best.
From a bathtub perch, to jump in was his quest.
Hair dryer blowing and combing he craved,
Of his aquatic habits, all visitors raved.

His kidneys started failing and on the blink.
Vomiting started by the side of the sink.
X-rays and surgery found a dangling glass,
Stuck in his stomach and could not pass.

Jack's trademark tweeds and neck ascots,
Stowed away Percy in his topcoat pocket.
This musical pair quite a scene they made,
Till the final days, when both were laid.

College professors are a special breed of cat unto themselves. Academia seems to attract individuals with great intellect and unique personal attributes. As a veterinarian, I was intrigued by their reasoning and approach to their animals, which seemed to live a nearly human life. I learned much about the personal lives and backgrounds of the academics who visited my veterinary office as they shared their pets and experiences with me.

Jack Graham was a tremendously accomplished clarinetist. His great friend was a triangular faced, Seal Point Siamese cat named Percy. He had been named after the fine Canadian-born band leader, Percy Faith. Jack was always very well dressed in tweed sport jackets and ascots. He taught music theory, performed in the symphony orchestra, and gave lessons to aspiring musicians. His wire-rimmed glasses and ruffled hair made this graying gentleman and his old kitty quite a distinguished couple.

Jack found Percy in the "pets for sale" column of the *Wichita Beacon*. He checked out the private residence from the street before making the decision to climb the steps and knock on the door. Upon viewing the tempting merchandise, he was hooked. The roly-poly, six-week-old Siamese kittens were irresistible. Three of the four chocolate points had been spoken for. The one who seemed to hold back from the roughhouse games that kittens play remained available. It was Jack's first choice, not even yet knowing that the three more rambunctious kittens were off limits.

Despite first appearances, Percy was far from laid back, and became a lover of listening to stereo music, particularly the clarinet and big band arrangements played by his professor-mate. Percy was also enthralled by Jack's thirty-gallon fish aquarium. The cat climbed to the shelf above which was warmed by a fluorescent light. He watched the fish and dipped his paw into the water to play with them. As a result, most of his daily water intake came from licking his wet paws. While sleeping on this shelf, Percy's dangling tail swished back and forth like a metronome. The fish seemed mesmerized by its continual slow movement and were drawn to the side of the aquarium to watch. Few fish have names, but musicians, it turns out, are also quite creative in this realm.

Jack's angelfish, black mollies, neon tetras, and gouramis had names like Benny and Goodman, Pete and Fountain, Jimmy and Dorsey, Woody and Herman, and Pee Wee and Russell.

Jack and I shared stories of our common backgrounds, both of us Kansans now living in near-neighboring Iowa. Though he had been raised as a "city kid," we always had pleasantries to share about our faraway childhood homes. Seeing Jack in his tuxedo on symphony nights only made his stature as a debonair and distinguished professor rise. To connect with Percy on Jack's level gave me a warm feeling of reward, thankful that God had given me this opportunity to help animals and people.

Percy was a rare cat that loved to take baths. Jack told me about Percy's unusual habit of jumping into the shower and getting thoroughly soaked while Jack was bathing. If Jack took a bath in the tub, Percy jumped up on the back of the rim and looked longingly, like he could not wait to jump in for a swim, and he would have done this in a split-second if it had been allowed.

The cat most preferred the walk-in shower. After his shower, he leaped up on a wing-backed wicker chair and onto the vanity counter to be dried off with a hand towel. To top off his grooming, he sat perfectly still while his "beautician" dried him with a hair dryer. This routine continued with Jack's daily schedule dedicated to this incredible feline's bathing fetish.

As I came to know Jack and Percy over many years, I was touched by Jack's great love for his old friend. Percy was eighteen years old and near the end of his life. The regal movements of this large-frame tom were slowing. Arching his back and purring relentlessly, he would pass back and forth under my hand like this trip to the vet was for the massage he had longed for.

Percy started vomiting shortly after the New Year. Many times, there is a surge in cat vomiting incidents after the Christmas season. It seems that some cats just cannot leave the tree ornaments, pine needles, and clear tinsel alone. Most of these objects can be ingested. However, these small pieces do not show up well on an x-ray. A foreign body is a potential diagnosis when a vomiting cat is presented after the Christmas holiday season.

As kidneys fail in cats, they are not able to excrete the urea nitrogen and creatinine as they filter the blood through the kidney's glomeruli. In Percy's condition, he would have felt nauseous and vomited sporadically, and since he had not bothered the Christmas tree in previous seasons, the ingestion of foreign material seemed unlikely. Fluid therapy was started by giving Percy lactated Ringer's solution under the skin. This is a means of making the body absorb more liquid. With this added volume of fluids flowing through the kidneys, the impurities of metabolism can be diluted and excreted in the urine. This subcutaneous fluid therapy was done three times each week for several weeks. It did seem that following the fluids, Percy appeared brighter in his eyes. They became less receded when his hydration improved. He continued to eat but not with much enthusiasm. Some days there was food in the vomitus, and other days it was just a yellowish phlegm. He was losing weight. Several x-rays were taken, and his abdomen was palpated often, but it never revealed any obstructions.

"Jack, it is unusual for a cat to want to eat when his kidneys are failing. His breath does not smell uremic. I can't feel anything in the abdomen. The blood tests indicate that the kidneys are not functioning well. There may be a cancer in the intestinal lining." I shared my diagnosis with Jack. His forlorn facial expression, so hoping that something could be done for his friend, showed me Percy's issue was taking a toll on Jack's health as well.

"I've been taking him to work with me under my overcoat, and he sleeps in a basket under my desk," Jack admitted. "He is so good, and he just lays there purring, snuggled under my jacket, knowing that it is probably against the rules to have a cat at school." Jack softly chuckled.

"No kidding," I laughed.

"As you know, I would do anything for him, Dr. Kenyon. If there was a chance of Percy getting better . . ." Jack looked at me with pleading eyes.

"I am to the point that we would need to do a surgical exploration of his abdomen to get a biopsy or see grossly if there is any obstruction or strictures anywhere," I offered. "This has been on my mind, but he is so weak. I have not wanted to put him at more risk."

After showing Jack diagrams of the abdomen and reviewing the x-rays one more time, we scheduled the surgery for the next morning. I gave Jack instructions to withhold food overnight. When they arrived the next morning, Jack looked even more disheveled. He handed Percy over to me, and I handed Jack a box of tissues. He said that he had not slept all night. He just held Percy and read books to him.

"If you would not mind waiting here in the reception room, I will perform the surgery immediately, and we'll have an answer in just a few short minutes," I told Jack. Cali, the receptionist, offered him some coffee to help with his fatigue.

I am always amazed when geriatric animals handle anesthetic so well. The lights and blips of the monitoring machine assure me that the body and heart are handling the sedation. Percy was laid on his back, and his legs were extended to the front and back and tied with surgical ties. The abdomen was prepped, and the mask, gown, and surgical pack were opened. Within minutes, I had opened the midline of the belly and started through the contents from the front to the back. I did not have to feel about for long, as I touched an object in the stomach. After packing off the greater curvature of the stomach with gauze sponges, I made a small incision into the mucosa and popped the object out through the opening with ease. I had found the answer to Percy's six weeks of vomiting and debilitating weight loss. The fifteen-millimeter, columnar, "dangly" glass piece from a small table lamp had caused all the problem. It was too big to go through the pylorus and into the intestine. It was too large to come back up when he vomited. Glass does not show up well on an x-ray because it is opaque. The stomach is far up under the rib cage, so it is nearly impossible to touch it and feel a foreign body with the fingers upon palpation through the body wall.

A few quick sutures were placed in the stomach tissue. I could not wait to tell Jack the good news. The abdominal wall and skin were sutured, and the anesthetic turned off. In only a few moments, Percy's eyes opened, and he was upright. He was wrapped in a warm towel and cradled in my arms. I hurried to the waiting room to hand him over to Jack and show him the glass piece. Jack gulped and said, "There was a desk lamp that had been knocked over a few months ago. Man, I thought all of the pieces had been replaced."

Alas, a missing glass piece had been found.

With tears running down his face, Jack embraced me, squeezing Percy between us with joy.

Percy lived two more years. Sadly, Jack became ill too and did not live much longer after that. They were a loving pair and gave totally to each other. I smile often when I think of that old Siamese rubbing affectionately on Jack's whiskered face.

Phoebe

Ode to Phoebe

'Tis said that color on chromosome is linked.
Was to stay in my room, just as she winked
A tortoiseshell beauty with talents unique.
Her personality and quirks were all quite boutique.

Perched on a shoulder, hours would stay.
Hide and seek with the poodle, the games they did play.
Her name was Phoebe, white patch on her chin,
As a princess this Tortie was pretty as sin.

Not much of a killer, the mice she would play.
Could hear a fly buzzing three rooms away.
A litter of kittens, half dozen in all.
Moved them daily, just down the hall.

Her girl off the college studying to be a vet,
Phoebe lay on the books, helping knowledge to get.
Along came a man, the husband to be.
Problems adjusting to a household of three.

Salivating started, a tooth it was thought.
The vet dentist found cancer on the tongue she had got.
Medication for pain, like a trooper to end.
Buried near Pixie, her poodle and lifelong friend.

"Mom, can I have a cat?" Carolyn pleaded. "I could keep her in my room and care for her every day. I will be so lonely upstairs with my sister going off to college."

Carolyn's mother resisted, yet again. "Honey, you know I am allergic to cat dander. I think it's best not to have a cat in the house."

Mothers do make sacrifices. There also are times when, with good reason, they make a compromise for a loved one. Carolyn's relationship with this three-month-old tortoiseshell who became her soulmate began early one morning at her summer job.

Carolyn had just received her learner's permit following a summer session in driver's education. She rose each morning at 5:30 without an alarm clock and scurried down for a breakfast of leftovers from the fridge, her choice of morning meal varying from tacos to pulled pork. She needed to be at the veterinary clinic to start the morning kennel chores by six o'clock. Carolyn loved this job, and feeding and caring for up to fifty dogs and cats required an early morning riser. The boarding and hospitalized patients would immediately start to bark and meow a chorus when the key turned in the lock to the door of the veterinary clinic. The long-time, veteran, veterinary assistant and caregiver would greet Carolyn when she arrived. The girl fed each dog and walked it on the adjacent vacant lot. Seven days a week, these morning routines gave this young animal-lover a large dose of education in animal care and behavioral training. In the reception area at the clinic was a retail and animal products section. A pet adoption cage there gave us an opportunity to showcase kittens who needed a home.

Kittens in the Midwest are born in April and October because female cats are seasonal poly-estrous. This means the queen ovulates with the changing of the length of the day. Since daylight starts getting longer in February and shorter in August, most of the nighttime "catting around" occurs in these seasons. It takes nine weeks, or sixty-three days of gestation (time in the oven), resulting in newborn kittens in April and October.

A spring crop of four littermates was brought to the vet clinic at closing time. They were farm kittens, and their mother had stopped feeding and nursing, trying to wean them. The farm had many cats already, so this quartet of two blacks and two tortoiseshell kittens was sent to us for adoption.

It is miraculous, but a fact, that hair color and a kitten's gender are on the same chromosome. Thus, hair color is a sex-linked characteristic. It is this receptor that causes calicos and tortoiseshell kittens to be females. A tortoiseshell female will also have an exceptionally soft hair coat. Their personalities are also unique.

The sun had just crested the horizon, and the stillness of the morning was broken. Upon opening the retail door to the clinic on this June morning, a chorus of meowing echoed throughout the pet adoption room. A flip of the light switch revealed a small herd of kittens climbing the black, wire display cage, begging for food and attention. The litter pan had ample deposits, and a zealous kitten had overachieved in trying to cover up, scattering gray clay litter throughout the cage and over the edges. Hanging like an acrobat, the most vocal kitten was a gorgeous tortie. She had a wisp of white on her chin that accented her distinctive, tricolored face.

Three hours of feeding, watering, cleaning cages, mopping floors, and washing the bowls and pans made Cinderella's jobs look easy. Anxious to get back to see the kittens, Carolyn at last hurried to the retail area to find that the kittens now had full tummies and were not quite as rambunctious. She reached in to rescue the little tortie who immediately used her claws to climb and scramble up a sweatshirt arm and perch on Carolyn's shoulder for a view of the surroundings.

The kittens' cage was cleaned, and a soft, pillowed, circular bed was placed in the corner. It immediately attracted all four of the curious kittens. They pounced over the edge and hid until the next one dared to scale the sides, only to bat each other on the faces and then scurry away. This game continued until their little bodies were exhausted and the battle ceased. The foursome then curled into the soft nest and became an entangled ball of sleeping kittens. Not an eye was open.

All morning long, the busy retail door was opened and shut. The electronic buzzer on the latch whined, announcing each entrance and exit. Grooming clients entered, and all the shaggy dogs stopped to sniff the kittens. Restrained by a precariously held leash, each dog tried to discern what this motionless mass could be. With an inevitable "Woof! Woof!" the mass of kittens came springing to life. Hissing, spitting, and arching their backs like Halloween scaredy cats, the kittens stood their ground, forcing the surprised mutts back, bewildered by this brave foursome.

By mid-morning, one of the blacks cracked open an eye, yawned, and stretched with her front leg draped over her siblings. Slowly, dreamtime ceased, and they were all awake with a stretch. They would prop their heads over the side of the bed like soldiers peeking out from a fox hole. Reenergized after their nap, they scampered off to play and use the gray gravel clay litter pan in the corner.

Carolyn checked in on the kittens frequently. All morning they were fast asleep. Finding them finally awake, she attached a pom-pom to a string and suspended it from the top of the cage so it dropped down into the enclosure. A game of tetherball ensued with the batting of the glittering piñata from one side to the other. All four kittens joined in the game. The tortie-calico with the white chin stood on her back legs and seemed to be the most athletic and adept at swatting the pendulum pom-pom. She would duck as her mates leaped to get into the action. Carolyn could not resist opening the side door and cuddling this special kitten.

"You are the prettiest kitty I have ever seen," she whispered to her new friend. "You are coming home with me and I'm going to call you Phoebe after an adorable princess from a book I am reading." It was destiny that brought Phoebe into Carolyn's arms that morning and for the next fifteen years.

That night, Phoebe rode in Carolyn's lap and went home with her. She was first confined to Carolyn's upstairs bedroom with food, water, and a large kennel with a soft, spongy, satin-covered bed. Since Carolyn's mother was allergic to cat dander, the promise was that Phoebe would stay in Carolyn's bedroom to avoid spreading the cat allergens into the rest of the large, three-story, Cape Cod style house in the woods. This plan worked for about one day, as Phoebe started reaching under the door with her tiny paws and meowing to be released from captivity.

Pixie, the family's brave, fluffy, black, six-pound, miniature poodle darted up the carpeted staircase to check out the intruder. She sniffed at these unusual little paws digging under the door.

Pixie thought, *How could this creature have come into my house without me being informed? And how could there only be one animal inside that room, when now there are four upside-down paws, playing and beckoning under the edge of that door?*

Carolyn went to work again early at the vet clinic. Phoebe had slept all night with Carolyn in her canopied bed. Nestled in the crook of her arm, the pair had slumbered since midnight. Leaving for work at predawn, Carolyn carefully placed Phoebe in her cage on a satin blanket, but purposely

135

did not close the cage door. Thus, the cat was out of the bag! The dog had been drawn to the action, and the brief confinement to the upstairs bedroom ended.

Carolyn had to be encouraged to take the cat off her shoulders while at the dinner table each night. When not playing "cat and Pixie" games, Phoebe was adept at batting a neon, Velcro ball across the hardwood floor. As it rolled toward her, she would leap in the air to avoid being hit. It was back and forth, with leaping and batting and chasing the ball until exhaustion resulted in another cat nap.

Kittenhood—the continual activity of a kitten playing with a ball, chasing a string, stalking a buzzing fly, and watching dust particles suspended in the air by the rays of sun—can fill a life with joy. And for a cat, how can it get any better than to eat, sleep in a girl's arms, and incessantly play?

There is no pill or shot that can keep kittens, or little girls for that matter, young. They grow up together and each page and chapter of life brings another adventure and new experiences.

Phoebe became a mother two years later, delivering a large litter of six kittens. Phoebe's huge midsection was finally relieved to show off her sleek physique again when the kittens were born under Carolyn's canopied bed. Suddenly this pampered tortoiseshell was transformed from kitty to coddling mother cat. Nursing six wiggling, crying babies can be a chore, even for a seasoned pro. In Phoebe's case, it was a psychological juggernaut. How to corral all six kittens to nurse at the same time was enough of a challenge, but leaving them for only a few minutes to eat, drink, and relieve herself was often put off as she licked and preened each of the half-dozen babies with all her motherly instincts.

The instinct of a mother cat is to protect their newborns from outsiders, and this trait was strong in Phoebe. If one of Carolyn's friends or even her brother peeked in to admire the brood, mother Phoebe picked up each kitten by the neck and moved them to a different location. She might move them under the bed or behind a chair in the hall. She had some attention problems, because a lonely kitten or two that had not yet opened its eyes might be left behind in the last bed. The muffled mewing brought Carolyn or her parents to the rescue.

A cat's genetics gives them an uncanny ability and awareness of the presence, smells, and faintest noises not heard by the human ear. Phoebe possessed these traits. She could spot a ladybug inching its way along the windowsill. She could sit still, entranced by the invisible object behind the woodwork, carefully repositioning her head from side to side to catch each vibration. Her intense face and piercing eyes would focus. Mice were her favorites, and few housewives are tolerant of these gray rodents with cute little ears. Phoebe, the great hunter, loved October when the golden leaves were falling and these little varmints squeezed their way through the smallest cracks in the foundation of the old house in the woods. She was in her element when one of these creatures dared to cross her radar. Careful not to penetrate the mouse's skin with her razor-sharp ivories, she played "cat and mouse" until her saliva soaked the mouse and it seemed to cry for mercy.

The plea for a kitty when her older sister went off to college at St. Olaf came full circle for Carolyn. With her senior year in high school coming to an end, dreams for new adventures pushed Carolyn to college. Phoebe, the shoulder riding, crook-of-the-arm sleeping, cat-and-mouse playing addict, and catnip "freak-out" princess was left behind with Carolyn's parents.

Phoebe paced the house most waking moments. Accompanied by her little poodle friend Pixie, they continued to play hide and seek. Crouching behind the door frame, each one in their own turn would walk unannounced through the doorway, only to have the other one jump straight up in the air, and the race was on. Sliding across the hardwood floor, cat and dog took turns being the pursuer and the pursued.

Because Phoebe only drank her water from the dripping faucet in the bathtub, the cascading trickle of this waterfall was provided full-time for her pleasure. A partial glass of milk left on the kitchen table would find Phoebe drawn to it like a magnet. Tilting her head to the side, she carefully dipped her paw into the white liquid and could empty a glass in no time.

Unbeknown to the parents, Phoebe had started taking her loneliness, frustration, and separation from her beloved Carolyn out on others by using the lush, deep-pile, white formal living room carpet to squat and relieve herself. It does not take an astute person with even a limited olfactory ability to pick up on the scent of cat urine on a warm autumn day. Banning Phoebe from all carpeted areas, intense and diligent cleaning of her litter box, and giving her more attention partially helped alleviate the piddling habit. Lured into believing that the problem was under control, it surfaced again with Thanksgiving, Christmas, and school breaks when Carolyn came home. The sorority girl with her incredibly devout kitty were inseparable on these home reunions. The carpet-piddling would start again after each home visit during Carolyn's undergraduate years in college, so the off-limits barricade would be placed in the doorway to the living room once again. This behavior problem is described as a psychosomatic response to the separation from Phoebe's soulmate.

While Carolyn was an undergraduate living in the Pi Beta Phi sorority house, Phoebe could not go to college with her mistress. However, the joyous day in May came when Carolyn was accepted into the veterinary college at Iowa State University. The two were at last reunited in a south-facing, second story apartment with an enclosed patio. A routine of sleeping, separating for class, sleeping in the warm sunlight beaming through the slider, running like a dog to greet Carolyn just home from class, dinner, and perching next to the books of homework on the table while Carolyn studied was Phoebe's schedule for the next amazing four years.

Eventually, a dreamy man came to visit. Phoebe was always leery of any outsider. She had just turned ten years old and did not willingly accept another human into her life. This handsome man, Christopher, stayed. Vet school graduation, wedding bells, and a move to a new townhouse came with some consternation. Phoebe did not like this new housemate and may have sensed that the feelings were mutual. She reverted to her old habit of using the lush carpet as her litter pan, much to the dissatisfaction of the new man in the house. This marking pattern was big trouble. Now living with two working adults, Phoebe's time of uninhibited attention and sleeping was disrupted. She was soon confined to a tiled bathroom while the couple was away. Phoebe was still allowed to sleep with Carolyn but had to be under a watchful eye during waking hours.

Carolyn began to notice an unusual salivation and wet lips with Phoebe. Now an accomplished veterinarian, Carolyn examined Phoebe's mouth for foreign materials. She suspected an infected tooth. Phoebe's gingiva was fire engine red, and a dental appointment was scheduled to have her teeth cleaned. Under anesthetic by the veterinary dentist, a soft medusa-head growth under her tongue and along the mandible was discovered. It resembled a small cauliflower shape. A biopsy revealed that it was a squamous cell carcinoma type cancer. It had invaded the soft tissue of the tongue and mandible and was deemed impossible to remove surgically. For the next six months, an oral medication called piroxicam was used to lessen the pain and some of the inflammation. Phoebe was a trooper in taking this chicken flavored medication each morning. Finally, ataxia and a seizure, indicating the cancer had spread to her brain, meant Carolyn had to say goodbye.

Having grown up together, sharing the joys of every journey, the two parted with a tearful hug and one last ride on the shoulders on a perfectly beautiful Indian summer day. The golden leaves of autumn were a stunning accent to this beautiful tortoiseshell with a wisp of white on her chin. She was buried alongside her great poodle friend, Pixie, under the large oak tree at the parents' home in the woods.

Salem

Ode to Salem

An abandoned tom, in the country was dumped.
Had a scratch on the head and one on his rump.
Luckily rescued by a kind special ed teacher.
Found a college girl to take this neat creature.

Named Salem, he was gun-metal gray.
Moved back home when school was out in May.
Disliked by Dad, an evil looking scowl.
Tried to pet him, but only a growl.

A lesson he learned, as only John did feed.
"No like me, then no food," he quickly did heed.
The strategy worked, they soon were bubs, the best.
Salem still intimidated any house guest.

Oh, a hunter he was, climbed many a tree.
Birds were not safe when he was free.
Like Sylvester and Tweety, with a bird in his mouth,
Feathered friends only safe when they headed south.

Whipped cream was his fav, the kind in a can.
Hearing the "whoook" sound, from anywhere he ran.
Suffered from crystals, could not be a wetter.
Surgery made a squatter out of this setter.

black cat . . . witches . . . unusual powers, magic, evil, mystery, sorcery . . . The word Salem conjures images of the 1600s Massachusetts trials and hideous attacks on some of the most unusual people of the times, but this cat with the name Salem had an unusual background as well.

A friendly gray male cat made roll call at the breakfast feast offered each morning by a rural veterinarian's wife along the county gravel road in rural Bremer County. Every morning, this special-education teacher supplied a smorgasbord for a dozen outdoor cats before she drove to the high school where she taught. Her husband helped spay and neuter them, though his patience was running thin with her attracting this large congregation. She was able to find homes for many of her adopted friends, and now she added this gray to the list. Luckily, the math teacher at the high school was moved by the wife's sad story, and luckily, the big gray cat went to live with a girl named Ann at her college apartment.

We will meet up again with Salem.

Meanwhile, I was called to a small ranchette. Or maybe I should call it a farmette, or at least a small acreage that had fields of corn behind the barbed wire fence in the backyard. The neighbor had a haphazard operation of nearly fifty milking goats. Their constant bleating and musky, odoriferous emanations were reminiscent of a backwoods type dwelling. There was a dairy in the distance where the morning echoes of the bellowing cows reverberated through the stillness before their trek into the dairy parlor. Pheasants cackled and crowed in the far grassy draws and pastures. Cats and more cats inhabited the outdoors of the small subdivision among the widespread houses along the dead-end, dusty gravel road.

I pulled up in the driveway on a Saturday afternoon in the red vet truck, not quite knowing the extent of the upcoming adventure. Saturday farm calls in a mixed animal practice were usually dedicated to small operations where the owners worked in town and only had Saturdays free to meet a veterinarian during daytime hours. A "mixed animal practice" can mean a backyard horse with a cough, a few bottle-raised calves with diarrhea, an anorectic pot-bellied pig, a cow with an injured horn, a small flock of sheep with sore mouths, an emu with a snotty nose, and—why not?—a herd of cats needing vaccinations.

I was met at the doorway by John—who turns out was Ann's father—a John Deere engineer who had stopped at the clinic a few days earlier asking if I could come out to vaccinate some cats. He had been referred by Janie, his neighbor. Janie had a habit of bringing cats into town to the clinic in the trunk of her car using a pillowcase with a string securing the top as a cat carrier. She just knew I would be willing to come out to the house to meet John's menagerie.

I greeted John when I arrived. "Good afternoon. I understand that you have some cats that you would like vaccinated?"

A very stoic John in his Saturday work Levis smiled. "Yes, I guess you could say that."

Having never met him before, there was something in his voice that struck me as cautious. We discussed the different vaccinations and decided that rabies and distemper were the best ones to use for his outdoor cats. If we worked it like an assembly line, we should be able to vaccinate a dozen or so cats.

"So where are the cats?" I asked, assuming they were all confined and ready.

John nonchalantly said, "Well, there are a few in the shed, but most of them are just out back where I feed them. I waited to feed them till you got here, so they should be hungry and pretty easy to catch."

"You mean we have to catch them?" I tried to shield my thoughts with my voice. This fifteen-minute stop was going to be at least an hour of fetch, capture, and trap a dozen or more cats that were appearing behind the scattered boards, saddles, and feed bales around the porous, rickety shed. Yes, "herding cats" came to mind, but I wanted to stay positive, knowing this stop had the potential of an all-afternoon roundup.

I drew up the vaccine for a dozen cats and followed John to the backyard. He started catching the easy, tamest ones first. Then it was "one-two" inoculation pokes under the skin at the back of the neck for the first innocent volunteers. It became instantly apparent that John had never been to a cat roundup before. When releasing each cat, it darted away from the surprise of the shots. The wiser ones were alerted that something was amiss and maybe this was not just a nice man who had brought them some extra treats at feeding time. John seemed to know which ones we had vaccinated, but before long, these cats all looked the same to me. After depleting the numbers around the food bowl, John casually said, "Now, there are a few more in the shed."

A few—this was good news. I carried the vaccination tote, and we opened the shed door. Two reasonably tame tabbies met us, and they were easy pickings. One-two and out the door they went. There was a pair of eyes glowing from the dark corner, cowering near the paint cans. John enthusiastically said, "There you are. I thought there was one more in here. He may be a little skittish. I trapped him in here last night."

Skittish heck! This little demon was a wild animal. With his leather-gloved hands, John got on his hands and knees to reach for the elusive cat. In one acrobatic leap, the skittish black streak bounded onto John's shoulder momentarily, hit all three shelves, and made it to the top, knocking dusty tools and nail cans to the floor. A crack of daylight at the top of the shed door was his next target. Without hesitation, he leaped for the door and, thank goodness, it sprang loose the trap. The cat was gone in a black streak by the time we peered out the door.

John seemed disappointed and dryly said, "Rats, I don't think I'll be able to catch him again."

"Yeah, John. You may have your work cut out for you trying to tame that little guy. But, if you do catch him, I would put him in one of Janie's pillowcases and bring him into the office."

After two hours of search and capture, I hurried out the driveway to try to make up the rest of the afternoon schedule. No blood, no bruises, no scars, but this roundup was one for the books!

I never saw the little black demon at the clinic, but John did stop in with another big gray cat. "This is Salem. He's my daughter Ann's cat. She moved to another apartment at Iowa State which didn't allow cats. So, I guess you could say he is my cat now. She said it's been a few years since he has had any vaccinations."

I breathed a sigh of relief thinking that at least this was not a wild cat and there were no pillowcases involved.

John explained where Salem got his name. As the story unfolded, this cat came to be called Salem from a TV show, *Sabrina, the Teenage Witch*, popular with college kids in the late '90s. On the show, Salem was a gray cat, cast as a mortal that had been changed into a talking cat by a witch.

Salem was not happy at our first meeting, and he was far from a talking cat. He had a scowling frown that suggested he disliked those in his presence. John confided that Salem had not been happy to come to live with him, and it took some time before the cat showed him any acceptance. And as it turned out, Salem's dislike for the veterinarian escalated each time he had to return.

***

Whoook! Whoook! was the sound of the whipped cream can. When it sounded, Salem came running "faster than a speeding bullet." This cat absolutely loved whipped cream.

"Where is the cat?" his human would ask. "I dunno," and out from the fridge came the chilled, frothy, aerosol dairy product. Myth or fact—that most cats are lactose intolerant never concerned Salem. Leaping up on the counter to the sound of the can, he was content to lick it straight from the white plastic nozzle. He'd take it off the top of a piece of pie or from a foamy squirt on his paw. If he was outdoors and the family was ready for bed, this was the lure to get him to come in so they could lock up the house for the night. John, at last, figured out how to be a popular guy with Salem by coating his evening desserts with dreamy whipped cream.

Salem loved watching the moon. His eyes glowed, emanating through the boughs as if from another world. He would remain statue-like, entranced in thought. Only an occasional flick of his whiskers gave him away.

There were many benefits to living on the outskirts of town with a large cropland in the backyard. Field mice and grasshoppers were never safe when the big gray cat was on the prowl. However, his favorite pastime was birds. They fascinated him. The flight, the chirping, and movement in a tree brought Salem to the scene. John watched Salem with amazement for his concentration and intense, slow-motion movement as he inched to the base of the magnolia tree. Since Salem had no front claws, he may have had a slight disadvantage in the hunt. Staring intently with only the tip of his tail twitching, he focused his radar on a bird. For Salem, the catch was the climax of the game. He was a "catch and release" cat, much like fishing or a no-kill shelter.

Sylvester and Tweety Bird could have taken lessons from Salem. On one occasion, John was slumbering on his deck and looked up from his book to see Salem, with head held high, come strutting toward him with feathers coming from both sides of his mouth. Dropping everything, John rushed down the steps to the hunter and pried open his mouth. To his astonishment, the freed bird fluttered and took flight.

***

Upon receiving a beep on my electronic pager from the answering service, I returned a call to John and his wife Mary. John answered the phone and said, "Doc, I hate to bother you, but Salem is having a problem. He keeps going to the litter box and yowling but nothing is coming out. I think he must be constipated. Can I bring him in tomorrow?"

Every veterinarian knows the symptoms, and this dear old wizard was not suffering from constipation, he had a urinary blockage. Of all the emergency calls, this was not one that could be put off until tomorrow. Without going into detail, and trying not to sound overly alarmed, I said, "Well, John, I believe he should be seen tonight. These signs may be that he is having a problem urinating. Can you meet me at the clinic in fifteen minutes?"

"I sure can, because he is one special cat, and I'd hate for anything to happen to him," John anxiously replied.

Salem came through the front door of the clinic in John's arms. His growling and shrieking yowl were different this time. The cat was clearly in intense pain. I touched his abdomen and sure enough, a hard, grapefruit-size urinary bladder was the giveaway that Salem had a blockage. Unplugging a male cat can be a breeze but it does entail a light anesthetic and a manipulation with a catheter to dislodge the blockage and relieve the bladder pressure. Each veterinarian has his or her own tricks and methods, but with a catheter in place, the bloody urine starts to flow. Struvite crystals along with cells from the irritated lining of the bladder and urethra usually form a matrix at the tip of the penis that stops the urine flow. The key word here is usually. This one was different. Small, oxalate, BB-sized round yellowish pebbles were packed like concrete in the urethra and tip of the penis.

Salem's condition required surgery. An amputation of the distal urethra and penis allowed for release and free flow of the dammed-up urine. This drastic procedure was necessary to save his life.

Salem was given intravenous fluids to restore his toxic ketoacidosis blood chemistries. We administered antibiotics and he was given some analgesics for the pain. An Elizabethan cone around his neck prevented him from chewing out his catheters, but further escalated his disdain for the veterinarian and staff.

In an attempt to alter the pH of the urine, making it more alkaline to change the cycle of the oxalate stones that continued to form, a change of foods and medications was prescribed. In Salem's case, even with his magical sorcery powers, these treatments did not prevent further recurrence of blockages. He was brought to the veterinary clinic four more times in the next two years with a blockage. Relieving his painful predicament required anesthetic, catheterization, and hospitalization with each recurrence.

Finally, the decision was made to relieve him from his pain and misery. John had held out hope and faith that every procedure would be able to give him just a few more days.

Salem was buried under the magnolia tree that had been his perch for surveying the landscape. Birds fluttered on the branches and landed, as if they knew they were safe from their old menace. The bleating goats, echoing from the distant dairy farm, and the early morning pheasants crowing were like music for the final resting place of the once great gray feline.

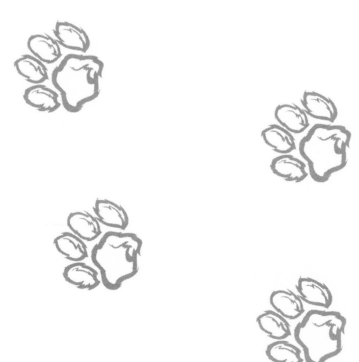

146

Sasha

Ode to Sasha

A cat named Sasha, is it Russian you say?
Came from the ghetto, no money did pay.
An ad in the paper, this kitten did come
A girl's secret, 'twas a gift for her mum.

From window to window, he followed the sun
Opened his eye to see a chipmunk run.
Under the Yule tree, he always would snug
Whether real or fake, he slept on the rug.

What was the sound, maybe hooves on the roof?
A kamikaze wing o'er the bed did swoop.
Papa sprang into action, even donning his hat
Surprised in the kitchen, found the cat on the bat.

Zipped through the house, crazy spells out of hell.
Except for a tooth, he always was well.
Ne'er to the vet, this cat ever did go
Saved his owners one pot of dough.

At the fire station, memorable lore
To find a lost cat, to alarm they tore.
With heat seeking lasers, they followed the sound
Poor Sasha they found, trapped underground.

Having spent a Rotary exchange year in Spain following high school, Monica Caruso was home at last. Spring had come and, unfortunately, her friends and classmates were all away at college. After greeting her parents and younger brothers, the home-again phase soon turned to long days alone on Pheasant Ridge. Her fun year in Barcelona with host families had given her a lust for an adventurous life. With both of her parents at work and the brothers in school, Monica longed for a companion. In Spain, her host family had a large Russian Blue cat which patrolled the house and veranda. Monica found an ad in the *Waterloo Courier* for free kittens. There was an address and phone number. Waterloo was more than fifteen miles away, but she called and arranged a time to adopt a kitten. In America, kittens seldom come with a price tag.

Monica only had a Waterloo city map from the phonebook. Her sense of north-south directions was limited, so finding the house on East Fourth Street was lucky. It was an older part of town and not somewhere an eighteen-year-old girl would venture alone after dark. There was no doorbell, so she knocked on the paint-chipped screen door. After the third time knocking, she was ready to flee the scene. Then the door creaked open. An older man dressed in dirty tan dungarees and a white muscle T-shirt asked what she wanted.

"Ah, you be the one. Well, there they are—take your pick."

Monica stepped inside the screen door onto the trash-cluttered porch. She surveyed the room and saw the four kittens sleeping in a ball. "I'll take that one with the yellow and white markings, if that is okay?" she cautiously asked.

The gruff bewhiskered man uttered, "Well, take it then, and I won't have you bringing that cat back neither!"

Monica scooped up the kitten and rushed toward the car that she had locked and parked on the street. Fumbling for her key, she tucked the kitten under her arm and quickly got into the car. Breathing fast, she could not believe the adventure. What was she to tell her parents when she came home with a kitten? Speeding away from this questionable, unsafe neighborhood, she devised a plan. Looking down at the kitten she whispered, "I'll just make you a birthday present for my mom."

The plot was set. The kitten with a cute red bow around the neck was secretly placed in a basket in the laundry room with the door shut. A note was taped to the sliding door. It said:

Roses are red
Violets are blue.
Happy Birthday Mother
This kitten is for you!
Love, Monica

When Monica's mother, Martha, came home after a long day of teaching at the high school, she was drawn to the note on the laundry room door. Finding Monica nowhere, she apprehensively opened it. What was not to like about a kitten with a red bow and its paws perched at the top of a basket? Mother Martha at first may not have been thrilled at the thoughtful surprise gift before her, but she said, "Now aren't you about the cutest thing!" With the kitten in her arms, she set off to find her daughter to thank her for her birthday wishes and the kitten.

Though Monica had gifted the kitten to her mother, and he was officially the family pet, it was Monica who came up with his name. Sasha, pronounced SAH-shuh, is a common name for boys in Russia, a nickname for Alexander.

Sasha was a hit with the family. They had never had an indoor pet before. The outside cats had just been nomads that came, stayed awhile, and disappeared into the night. Hawks, owls, raccoons, and foxes all battled for dominance outside their house snuggled in the woods along the banks of the Shell Rock River.

Coming into the house from the garage, one entered the laundry room. This became Sasha's official bedroom at night. It was outfitted with food, litter box, and a cat bed. With the sliding door closed, he was safe from wandering outside. For several nights, he meowed and cried in protest and loneliness.

When Sasha got older, he was able to jump up on top of the washer and dryer. He quickly was found sleeping in the laundry basket. From that day forward, this laundry basket became Sasha's bed.

After family time in the evening and the ten o'clock bedtime hour, Sasha would voluntarily head for his lair. If the slider had been accidently closed, he meowed in protest until someone came and let him in for the night.

** **

Martha's visiting brother, Jim Johnson, happened to be a veterinarian. He performed the delicate surgery on the kitchen table, and Sasha became an "it"—a neutered male. Also missing when it was over were his front claws. He was not allowed outside, although he occasionally made an exploratory jaunt when the door was ajar. Invariably, after this brief exploration in the outside world, he was welcomed back in the house and would start immediately "ralphing up" green grass.

Cats seem to have an internal button in them that sets off a neurological trigger to periodically explode and race around the house. Sasha was at it again. Three times up and down the circular staircase he would race. Darting from the carpeted living room, he would hit the wooden floor. Putting on the brakes, he skidded to a stop against the sofa. Out of breath, he would casually lick at his sides as if to say, *Who me? You didn't see anything, did you?*

Monica's father was Ivan. He was an architect. His design work and consultations for community projects and school buildings took him out of town at nights for important meetings with reviewing boards. On one such night, he arrived home at midnight from a meeting at Algona over one hundred miles away. When he came in from the garage, he flipped on the lights and looked into the laundry room to check on Sasha, who lifted his head with yellow reflections of his retinas shining like neon lights in the dark.

Ivan retreated to the bedroom and had just turned off the closet light. He crawled into bed and pulled up the sheets when a swishing sound came across the darkened room, then a second swishing. A third one came as he fretted over what this noise might be. Martha was awakened by his cold feet and at the fourth sound, she screamed, "What was that?"

Tired and unflappable, Ivan mumbled, "It was just probably just a bat."

"A bat! A bat!" she screamed. "*Just a bat*! You've got to go get it! And I mean now!"

Ivan reluctantly jumped into action. Stepping into his slippers, flipping on the light switch, he mumbled as he headed into the dark unknown to become a bat man. Upon reaching the kitchen, he found Sasha smiling like a Cheshire cat. In the middle of the floor, Sasha had the bat pinned with both paws, down for the count. Mr. Bat was scooted into Ivan's hat and carried out the door to fly away into the starlit night.

"Now I can finally get a peaceful night's sleep," Ivan mumbled to Sasha.

The Pheasant Ridge family home was meticulously constructed by Ivan and Martha. They had built it board by board, nail by nail, and the husband-and-wife team did all the drywalling, sanding, painting, and varnishing of the additions. Finally, it was time to add the master bedroom suite and the cut was made into the adjacent south side of the house. Work had to be done on weekends as their day jobs occupied them during the week. The crawl space was under the house and the entrance under the new bedroom was exposed. Sasha had been a great observer and accompanied Ivan into the chasm. Curiosity may not have killed the cat, but it surely did cause him to go on a five-day fast, as the reader is about to learn.

With Sunday night's last hammering and sawing completed, Ivan, on his hands and knees, crawled back out from under the cob-webbed, damp crawl space with his flashlight leading the way. The trap door was closed, and another project was completed until next weekend.

That night at bedtime, they couldn't find Sasha. Ivan, wondering if the cat may have stayed behind in the crawl space, ventured back in to look for him. Using his searchlight and calling for Sasha, he found no sign of the aging cat.

For the next three days, the family called for Sasha. They investigated the crawl space numerous times and started to worry that he had slipped outside and was gone. Finally, on the fourth day, a muffled meow was heard under the house. Ivan searched the crawl space again, calling for him with the light doing reconnaissance, but the mystery continued. Finally, Martha called the fire station in town. "I know this is maybe not a high priority, but I have always remembered the children's books where the firemen with their ladders came to help the little girl reach a kitty in a high tree."

Answering the call, firefighter Gene Walmsley said, "Yes, and we still do that on a rare occasion. How can I help you?"

"I know this is an odd request, but we have lost our cat in the house. He's been gone all week. I've heard that you have a heat seeking device that can locate a warm spot, like a body or a hot ember. Do you think you would be able to come and see if my cat is here beneath the house?" Martha pleaded.

Trying to control his laugh, Gene said, "Sure we could do that. In fact, we could come out right now. Where do you live?"

Relieved, Martha asked if they might just come in a car rather than arrive in a truck with all the sirens blaring.

In a matter of moments, the detector was flashing red over a spot under the floor. Martha directed the firefighters to the crawl space. Upon opening the door for what seemed the umpteenth time, flashing his beacon, the firefighter spotted a slightly hungry, embarrassed, and greatly happy orange and white kitty darting to the open door. A successful rescue for all!

The next day, Martha bought four pizzas and two liters of pop and rang the doorbell at the local fire station. She handed the stack of pizzas to the firefighter who answered to share as a thank you for the heat-seeking mission. He said, "Sure, why don't you come on in and give it to them yourself?" Martha was directed around the massive fire engines to the lounge where four firefighters were gathered. She was introduced. "Guys, this is the cat lady we told you about." The firefighters laughed and the saga of Sasha, the cat lost in its own house, was recounted again.

In his seventeen years, Sasha was one healthy cat. Though with Martha's brother, a veterinarian, and myself as frequent social guests at the family home, the very skimpy vet expenses were always kept to a minimum.

One day, hearing that Sasha may have had something caught in his mouth, I was asked to look in on this old friend. There it was, sticking straight out at a 90-degree angle from the side of the cat's mouth. Gingerly lifting his lip, I barely touched this protruding canine tooth and it fell into my hands. It had rotted off at the root, and this old laundry room, crawl space cat had not protested in pain, nor had he missed a meal. Upon lifting the lip on the other side, the other canine tooth was wiggled out with ease, and no blood came from the socket.

I commented, "Sasha, I'm sure glad this was a snap, because I doubt your mom has dental insurance on you." Laughter and smiles were exchanged with the family.

This old cat with a Russian name lived for two more years in his retirement. Until his last days, he greeted his dear family every morning and evening, sitting regally in his laundry room windowsill perch.

Slippers

Ode to Slippers

He had white paws which looked like spats.
To school and church, and places like that.
Known around town, this one named Slippers.
Was groomed with a vacuum, never with clippers.

This cat visited people, home through a cat door.
Myrtle across street, even added one more.
When at her house, the curtains were drawn.
Stayed out at night, came home before dawn.

Walked up the aisle, followed family to church.
Went to a pub, on a bar stool he perched.
Went home with a drunk, many miles away.
Answered ad in the paper, the owners did pay.

To the bait shop each morning, was treated with fish.
Loved rides in the car, any time he wished.
Used the crosswalk, principal's desk at school
Up two flights of stairs, kids thought it was cool.

Followed a hearse, the casket was wood.
Waited outside asleep on the hood.
At Slippers' passing, the town respects were paid.
In the Gillespies' back yard, his body was laid.

Bustopher Jones is not skin and bones—
In fact, he's remarkably fat
He doesn't haunt pubs—he has eight or nine clubs,
For he's the St. James Street Cat!
He's the Cat we all greet as he walks down the street
In his coat of fastidious black . . .
And we're all of us proud to be nodded or bowed to
By Bustopher Jones in white spats! . . .
"The Cat About Town," by T.S. Eliot

Though the setting is not as regal as London, another cat with spats was beloved by all in this small lakeside community in Central Minnesota, USA. Slippers, by name, he wore a black suit with white paws and tummy. He was found on a farm by Keith who had just picked up his fishing buddy. This black and white cat was so friendly, Keith could not resist bringing him home. The cat willingly jumped in his fishing car, a dusty Oldsmobile station wagon.

The Gillespie family of four lived at the time in Osakis, Minnesota. It was a farming community about two hours northwest of the Twin Cities. Keith was a school principal. His wife, Doris, and two children, Brad and Diane, were swinging on the porch when the Olds came up the driveway. Keith rolled down the window, smiled, and said, "You are not going the believe what I caught today." He opened the car door and out strolled a strikingly confident cat. Its long white whiskers accented its black face. His white paws stepped into the new yard and into the Gillespies' hearts for the next nineteen years.

Doris exclaimed, "He is just a spitting image of a cat my sister, Donna, had growing up as a young girl on our farm in Iowa. We loved him so much and called him Slippers!" And so it was that this cat was named Slippers.

Slippers made a visit to the local vet and had his boy surgery. This did not stem his instinct of traveling the neighborhood and meeting everyone with his outgoing personality. Doris learned quickly when trying get him inside that calling "Here Kitty, Kitty" seemed to fall on deaf ears. But calling, "Slippers, Come!" brought this white footed guy running from a block away.

The Gillespies lived on a corner lot across from the Lutheran church and adjacent to the grade school. Slippers watched the activity and cars along the street that came and went. He stayed on the sidewalk and followed the kids to school. He observed them only crossing the street at the crosswalk. He thought, *This must be the only way to get to the other side.*

Sundays also brought activity and cars parked along his street as families came to church. In the warm summertime, the church left the front doors propped open to allow for cross ventilation and cool air movement. Slippers had no sooner come to his new home than he, too, thought he needed to go to church. Sitting on the front steps, he watched his family leave to walk across the street and enter the church. The Gillespies sat in a pew near the front. They heard snickering and chattering behind them just before the service began. In strolled the innocent sinner, Slippers, in his Sunday best. He walked up the aisle like he was an usher. The congregation watched as the principal's wife slid out of the pew. They had heard of church mice, but this was the first church cat that they could recall. Doris retraced the steps with Slippers in her arms, down the long aisle just as the choir started singing the introit *Holy, Holy, Holy.*

※ ※ ※

Much like Mary's little lamb, Slippers thought he needed some schooling. He frequently went to the crosswalk, ran across the school grounds, up two flights of stairs, went to the principal's office, and jumped up on Mr. Gillespie's desk. Yes, even in Minnesota, it was against the rules to have a cat at school.

Keith would yell to the school secretary, "June! Would you please call my wife to come get Slippers?" Doris had to retrieve Slippers routinely from the principal's office. Slippers acted like this was his way of seeing the kids and helping them at school.

A convenience of living in a small town was that walking uptown was easy for appointments or shopping. Doris had walked to Dr. Lechband's dentist office for work on a tooth. She was in the waiting room, looking out the tall, decorative picture window, and caught a glimpse of Slippers sitting outside with his paws on the dentist's front door. She hurried outside to assure Slippers that she was okay. On the walk home they went by the bait shop along the shore of Lake Osakis. A man was sweeping the sidewalk and greeted them. "Hey, is that your cat? He comes here almost every morning. I usually treat him with a little fish. I hope that is alright?"

Doris smiled and introduced herself. "Yes, he is our cat. His name is Slippers. He has never met a person he doesn't like. He loves to visit everyone, and all seem to adopt him as their neighborhood cat."

❊ ❊ ❊❊

Seldom an event in town happened without Slippers in attendance. On a chilly November morning after the kids had gone to school, Doris noticed from the front window that a hearse had pulled up for a funeral at the church. The flowers were unloaded, and a casket had been rolled through the front doors. She had not noticed that Slippers was watching the gathering and those coming to pay their last respects. When the funeral was over and the casket came back out the front doors, there was Slippers curled up sleeping on the warm hood of the hearse.

Like Eliot's Bustopher Jones, many nights Slippers frequented the local pub in town called the "Do Drop In." Slippers thought, W*hat a friendly place. No matter what time I get here, I am always treated like one of the regulars and given a treat.* He even had a stool at the bar where a patron would lift him up, so he had a better view.

One night a man who was having just one last beer said to Slippers, "You know cat, why don't you come home with me. My kids would love a nice kitty like you." The suds were still running down the sides of the stein when he secretly snatched Slippers from his stool and hid him under his coat as he paraded out the swinging front door. When Slippers did not show up for breakfast the next morning, the Gillespies wondered just what kind of mischief he was up to. After three days of searching and inquiring around town, this vagabond kitty was officially declared AWOL. Doris had tracked his last known appearance to the tap room. Slippers had just vanished.

One week later, the newspaper had a notice in the lost and found column:

```
Friendly white footed cat.
Accidentally came here.
Pay for this ad and he is yours.
```

The city constable, who had been alerted of the disappearance of Slippers, brought the paper to Doris and showed her the lost and found notice. Doris called the number in the ad. Sure enough, the description fit, and it was none other than her beloved Slippers. She gathered her purse, jumped into her car, and set out on the rescue mission thirty miles away. She bailed out Slippers and paid the five dollars for the newspaper ad.

Slippers was so glad to see her, he ran to the car to go home. After this incident a new, light-reflecting collar was placed on the cat's neck. It had a round reflector that said SLIPPERS GILLESPIE and had the family's phone number.

❋ ❋ ❋

Keith struggled at times finding the perfect teaching job. He moved his family often after another two- or three-year principal position. The final move brought Slippers back to Keith's and Doris's native state of Iowa. Keith was again in a new principal's office, and Doris had gone back to teaching third graders at the nearby town of Livermore. Slippers packed up and rode into the next town without missing a step. The family watched in amazement as he scouted out his new surroundings. In just a day or two, they were confident that Slippers recognized his new digs and watched him venture off to find new friends.

Ten-year-old Diane walked uptown to look for Slippers on a Saturday morning. She found him in the newspaper office where he went often to check on city business. With Slippers in her arms, Diane walked past the flower shop. A man who was outside watering the plants along the sidewalk barked at this little girl carrying a cat, "Hey, Is that your cat? He has to be the one that got my cat pregnant!" Wearing her knee-patched jeans and with braided pigtails, Diane's face flushed as she stood her ground and looked straight at the man with the water hose and said indignantly, "Mister, that is not possible, my Slippers has been fixated!" She could not wait to get home to tell her mother that Slippers had been accused of such an injustice by the flower shop man.

Myrtle was an eighty-year-old spinster lady living across the street from the Gillespies. She had no pets but developed an immediate affinity to white-footed Slippers. Using her cane to get to the door, she let Slippers in whenever she found him sitting outside. Slippers went nearly every day to visit. She let him sleep on her bed with a cozy chenille cover. Young Diane came to retrieve the cat one time, and Myrtle greeted her, "He is sleeping now. When he wakes up, I'll send him on home."

She created a signal for the owners that when her front curtains were pulled shut, it meant Slippers was there. When the curtains were opened, Slippers was away.

One day, Myrtle was hanging clothes on the line when the lady next door yelled at her, "Would you come get your pesky cat? He is sitting under my bird feeder harassing all of my beautiful finches." Myrtle didn't flinch as she replied, "Genevieve, you haven't said a word to me in years, and now it's this cat's problem that he is only doing what cats like to do. I strongly believe that Slippers would not harm a fly, much less your plentiful gold finches." She called Slippers, and he came running. She carried him back home to the Gillespies and slipped him in the back door.

❄ ❄ ❄❄

Keith loved to go to estate auctions and find antiques. At one such sale, he raised his hand and bought a clock for $30. The auctioneer said, "Sold to the man in the red sweater." The sale spotter called out, "Your last name sir?"

Keith yelled back, "Gillespie!"

The town newspaper editor, standing behind Keith, tapped him on the shoulder and asked, "You aren't Slippers Gillespie's dad, are you? If so, he often comes down to the newsroom and sits on my desk watching all of the action at the office. I give him a fish treat, which may be the reason he comes in so often to check on the news."

If Slippers had a weakness for anything, it was fish. It started when Keith first put on his fishing vest and Bass Pro hat. Slippers followed him to the car and sat by the trunk waiting for Keith to load the tackle box, nets, and rods and reels. Slippers begged to ride along. The fishing trip was for guys only, but Slippers came running when the car pulled into the garage later that day and sat by the trunk for any fish scraps that would be coming his way. Standing in front of the upright Amana, Slippers meowed, *I know you have fish in there.* The meowing continued until one member of the family broke down and opened the fridge to give him a sliver of the fish fillets. It was remarkable that when the last of the fish shavings were gone and there wasn't more fish in the refrigerator, he stopped sitting in front of the door. The meowing and begging ceased, and he was off to Myrtle's or another fish fry table in town.

When the Gillespie's garage door was opened, Slippers was there, ready to go. If he was ignored, he leaped up on the hood and stared right into the windshield, pawing the glass and meowing, *Hey, did you forget me?*

The ice cream run was a favorite ride. He scampered in through the driver's side door and straddled the front passenger seat like he was mounted in a saddle. If the car dared to leave without him, he would dart to the Dairy Queen a few blocks away to make sure he was included for a few licks of soft serve. Doris had to clean the felt roof lining of the car more than once while the kids were holding their cones high to keep Slippers from eating more than his share.

On cleaning days, the Electrolux canister vacuum rolled out of the closet. Slippers knew the noise and it brought him running. He craved being vacuumed. The vibration and sucking of his hair coat, lifting every hair like static electricity, was like a day at the spa for Slippers. He wiggled with joy when his whole tail was sucked up into the wand. Needless to say, Slippers never had a hairball issue. When school friends visited, they begged to have Brad and Diane show off the cat-vacuuming routine. Slippers thought, *This is no big deal, but if they think it's cool, I'm all in!*

✵ ✵ ✵

Brad and Diane graduated from high school and were off to college. Slippers moped and paced the house. He checked their bedrooms, hoping to find them. Doris tried to give him more attention and included him in any car trips. With Doris away teaching school all day, Slippers came and went from the house, almost like a guardian cat. He sensed weekends, because he would stay home all day and did not roam or go exploring for a handout.

Slippers was a lover, not a fighter, and was able to walk away from any street cat skirmishes. Doris was not known for her singing voice, but Slippers did not care. She listened to the oldies station and especially to the music of the big bands like Glenn Miller. The station manager at KHBT was an acquaintance. His wife liked big band music too, so he played it frequently for his wife and Doris, and for Slippers, who swayed while Doris warbled.

Slippers started losing weight, and his shiny hair coat started to lose its luster. His appetite, even for fish, was greatly diminished. Dr. Harmon was the family's veterinarian. He was an elderly gentleman and had been amused every time Slippers came to the vet clinic, which hadn't been very often until the cat's later years. Dr. Harmon was consulted and prescribed a pink liquid antibiotic called Amoxicillin.

One morning, Doris had the radio blasting and the Beatles were strumming, *"Yesterday."* When the record stopped, Doris heard a cat crying. She went to the window and saw Slippers on the driveway. Doris put on her housecoat and hurried out to find Slippers lying still with shallow breathing. She carried him into the house and put him in his bed downstairs. She called Dr. Harmon's office, and he advised giving Slippers some more of the pink medicine. She called Diane who was back at school at Iowa State to tell her that Slippers was dying.

"Mom, I'm coming home. I only have one class this afternoon, and it is just a recitation. I want to say goodbye." The University in Ames was about eighty miles away. When Diane pulled into the driveway, Doris met her with tears in her eyes, said nothing, and held her daughter in her arms. Slippers had passed away.

Smokey

Ode to Smokey

Briars, brambles, and cockleburs too,
Found at the shop of an Amish woodworking duo.
She offered them a deal as a bargaining chip,
Finish the sleigh, and the cat will ship.

She tried to find him a home.
But they all worried he would roam.
After a shave down, he looked like a Maine.
Groomed himself daily, then the hairballs came.

Had a problem with piddling, yowling in pain.
Took to the vet, unplugged the crystals came.
Ne'er sick again, 'cept for a rotten tooth.
His buddy a Pyreenes, a big white 'galoot'.

Nattered and chattered, while perched at the sill.
Cleaned out the mice, but seldom would kill.
Dipped his food in water and ran like a dog.
With the lady in bed, they slept like a log.

The Amish in America date back to 1730. They came from Switzerland, Germany, and Holland. They were farmers and Anabaptist Christians who brought their simple life and family-centered conservative beliefs with them. They had large families and their population grew. There are over 150,000 Amish in America today. The largest populations of Amish are in Pennsylvania, Ohio, and Indiana. However, as many as twenty-four other states have settlements for various orders of the Amish. The guiding principles of the Order—in German, *Ordnung*—vary with the degree of conservative beliefs. One of the more conservative Orders is found in northeast Iowa, centered around the community of Hazelton.

Here, all farming is done with horse-drawn equipment. The men and women wear traditional, dark clothing of homemade dresses, trousers, bonnets, and shirts with no collars, lapels, or pockets. They wear no makeup or adorning jewelry. They do not have electricity, telephones, televisions, radios, or automobiles. All travel is by horseback or horse and buggy. The women wear dresses with either a cape or apron, and they do not cut their hair. They wear it braided or in a bun under their head caps. The men are clean-shaven until they get married and then they grow beards. No mustaches are allowed. Their trousers have suspenders and no pockets, cuffs, or belts. Since there are no buttons on their shirts or trousers, they are secured by hooks. Outside the community they are often referred to as Hookies. They believe in humility, close families, and a simple lifestyle that avoids ornamentation.

Horse traders, tack and equipment salesmen, and buggy makers all head for the Waverly Midwest Horse Sale, in Waverly, Iowa. This two-day auction is held each spring and fall. All breeds of horses are sold, but it is recognized as the largest draft horse sale in America. Belgians, Percheron, Shires, and Clydesdales are sold and traded by Amish and horse aficionados from all over the Midwest. Saddle makers, leather tack suppliers, and Amish tradesmen peddle their wares at this horse sale spectacle. The Yoder brothers, Orva and Alvin, are known for their buggy-making, but also repair carts, sleds, and farm equipment. They have buggies and tack for sale ringside.

Sam Zubak, known as a horse-lover and an animal rescue magnet, was raised on horses and had owned at least one horse for more than fifty years. She also had a nineteenth century horse-drawn sleigh that had been in the family for more than 100 years. She met the Yoders at the Waverly sale and told them of her desire to update the sleigh with leather upholstery and recondition the wood runners, seat, and hardware. Orva Yoder, tugging at his suspenders and studying this pretty, blonde horse lady, gave directions to his farm.

Orva was stoic, with eyes shifting back and forth toward his somber-faced brother, Alvin. Being a tradesman, Orva did not promise instant results and reserved the right to look at the project before committing his time and effort to restoration of the sleigh.

This was a green light to Sam. The following Saturday, she loaded the sleigh in the back of a trailer and tied it down carefully with straps. She drove about an hour on this late fall morning, to Edgewood in northeast Iowa, north of Hazleton. She drove on the Amish Boulevard, which features small roadside stands and stores selling fruits, breads, carpentry items, and horse equipment. Apples, pears, peaches, squash, and pumpkins were stacked high for the many city-folk shoppers to purchase. Upon arriving at the Yoder farm, she found Orva and Alvin working in their outdoor woodworking shop. Orva remembered their meeting from the week before. He and his brother examined the sleigh and said, "Ya, this is a nice sleigh. When was it last used?"

Sam explained, "I used to ride in it with my grandpa when I was little, maybe forty years ago, and it was pulled by a little Shetland pony named Prince."

Orva rubbed his chin and beard with his hand and looked at the sleigh for a moment and replied, "Ya. Interesting. Well, all the upholstery is dried and cracking and needs replacing. This runner pole is broken, and the side braces are in really bad shape."

"Yes, I realize that, but can you repair it?" Sam asked.

With his arms crossed under his suspenders he teased, "Ya, I can make it look new, but its gonna take a bit."

Sam knew that "awhile" or "a bit" to the Amish was open-ended and meant no definitive timeline. "Great, that is all I need to know. Just make it look new. I am very anxious to have it restored—it was my great-grandfather's first sleigh. Is it okay for me to check back with you? Just tell me when." She prodded for a commitment.

"I'd say give it a couple of months, should be done." Orva fielded the request but gave no date to check back with him. "Me and my brother will get right on to it in time," he winked at Alvin.

Sam volunteered with the spring and summer riding classes at the Iowa School for the Braille on weekends. She had a busy schedule with her John Deere employment travels internationally, so Sam put the sleigh repair to the back of her mind. It had been months since she had dropped it off at the Yoder farm, and she had not heard a word from them. She drove to the Edgewood farm on a Saturday to see if Orva was finished with the refurbishment. Hoping for the best, but prepared for the worst, she was relieved to find Orva at home during the busy, fall harvest season. The family had a large roadside stand selling fruits and vegetables. She discovered that nothing had been done on the sleigh during the ten months it had been with them.

A pitiful, meowing cat came up to her while she was talking with Orva. It was covered with cockleburs that were matted to the skin. "Oh, you poor kitty, you look so miserable. Can you pull any of the burrs out of him?" she queried.

"Oh, he's just a mangy old cat that showed up. He wants to come in the house. He even got in once and jumped on the table, and my wife shooed him out with a broom," Orva said. "I suppose you're here for your sleigh. Well, me and my brother not got to it yet. We've been quite busy you see. Why don't you take that old cat with you and check back with me in about a month?"

"I have cats of my own and don't know what I'd do with another one. Tell you what, I'll be back in two weeks, and if the sleigh is done, I'll take the cat too," Sam offered.

"Can't do! How about three weeks?" Orva bargained. The repair work at least had a deadline.

Three weeks later, again on a Saturday, Sam drove the sixty miles to pick up her sleigh. Much to her chagrin, Orva informed her that it was not quite ready. The Irish in her blood was nearing the boiling point when she spotted the poor old cockleburred cat that now appeared to have all of the burrs removed. He still had about an inch of solid, matted hair, but did look somewhat more comfortable. Orva tried to pawn off the cat again, but true to her convictions, Sam refused. She gave Orva one more week to complete the sleigh. The following Saturday, the beautifully refinished and refurbished dark, burgundy-seated sleigh looked like it had just come from the original maker. It was loaded into the pickup and the Amish cat crawled into a pet carrier to go home with Sam.

❊ ❊ ❊

169

Sam made an appointment at the veterinary clinic for neutering and to have the Amish cat shaved to the skin to remove the mats. Upon retrieval, this now-clean cat looked like a Maine coon. She named him Smokey for the color of his undercoat and skin.

Sam tried three different relocations for Smokey. A lady from Brandon took him home but returned him because he had beaten up all her other cats. The second home was a lady who was going to put Smokey in a cage in her basement. The third and last resort was to take him to the animal shelter, where she was given no promise that he would not be put to sleep if they could not place him.

That's how Smokey came to live as an indoor cat with Sam.

He took to indoor living like a cat to tuna. His beautiful, silky hair grew out to about an inch in length. He accepted plastic caps placed on his front claws to prevent him from shredding all the furniture, and he adapted to a scratching post for his instinctive moments of deep concentration and shredding a stationary object. Smokey's tail was like a flag in the wind. It stood straight up, and the tannish tip pointed forward with distinction.

At bedtime, Smokey started showing up in the bedroom. He jumped onto the bed, waiting for Sam to get into the reclining position. Sleeping on her left side, Smokey slept in the notch formed behind Sam's knees. Once in place, he scrunched himself forward and back to have all his hair lay flat. For the next fifteen minutes, he meticulously washed his face and ears and groomed his belly and legs before falling asleep. With the first light of day, he was up and biting Sam's nose to get her up for her workday. Because of Smokey's persistent cleaning of himself, regular cigar-shaped hairballs were found under a coffee table where he would "ralph" them to relieve any stomach impaction.

What a life for a matted, Amish, Maine coon! It seemed to be too good a story. Then, Max, a huge, half white Pyrenees/half Merino sheep dog came into the house to live with them. Max had also come from the Amish. Sam was at an auction where a bearded man was selling furniture. The auctioneer threw the audience a curve. He brought in a huge, white, supposedly pedigreed pup for sale. He was asking 500 dollars, but no one bid on him. Following the auction, the Amish man approached Sam as she had been eyeing the gorgeous puppy. He again tried to sell the pup, to which she said, "Well, maybe I would give you ten dollars." The man immediately said, "Sold." While reaching into her pockets, Sam was pulling out one-dollar bills. When no more were found, she reached deeper and started finding nickels and dimes. With the help of a few onlookers, she managed to scrape together $9.50 and this pup named Max was hers.

Max grew quickly into a 100-pound dog. He lived in Sam's cozy horse barn with four horses and a donkey. During a particularly harsh cold spell, Sam brought Max into the house. At first, he howled to go back outside. On the second night, the big lunk decided living in the house was not too bad and the die was cast. There was only one hurdle to overcome. The cat!

This huge ball of fur seemed to find Smokey's presence threatening. The cat had seen the snow-white monster out in the yard while perched on the windowsill. He thought, *I now have to live with a dog in my house?* Yet, Smokey tried to make friends and circled Max as he slept on the floor. He reached out with his paw at the switching, smoky-white tail. Then a sharp "haah" and the cat retreated under a chair.

Several days had passed when Sam returned home from work to find Smokey with glazed eyes and unable to move. The cat made a deep, throat-rattling gurgle and screamed when touched. All the way to the vet's office, Sam talked to Smokey. "I missed you last night. I should have known something was wrong when you didn't come to bed with me. I thought you were just preoccupied with Max. This is all my fault."

Smokey did not move, but his body twitched with each bump the car hit in the road. The young doctor, showing empathy, reported, "Smokey, you have a urinary blockage. Your poor bladder is the size of a baseball and as hard as a rock. You'll have to spend the night with me and get a catheter placed to relieve the pain and pressure in your bladder."

All the way home that night, Sam blamed herself for not noticing Smokey's symptoms earlier. Was it the dog? Was it stress? Was it the food? How could crystals in the urine form such a matrix and cause a blockage? Over and over, she mulled the reason for such a sudden illness.

Two days later, Smokey was able to come home. He was still weak and had been placed on a special veterinary diet to prevent further buildup of the sharp-edged triple phosphate crystals which caused the blockage. Max greeted them at the door and seemed to sense that Smokey had been sick. He looked at the shaved leg where an intravenous catheter had been placed. He sniffed at Smokey's back end and picked up an unusual odor from the medical procedure which had been performed.

From that day forward, Smokey and big Max were bunkmates. Where Max went, this big teddy bear Maine coon with his tail held high in the air followed. The mutual respect persisted. Max

171

enjoyed the big cat's ability to roll over on command, his ability to jump and catch a fly, and the way he would lay on his back, sprawled out with all four feet spread widely apart.

When Max died of cancer, Smokey grieved and stalked the house, looking for his friend. He stopped eating and stopped talking to Sam. He started drooling and parked himself on the couch. When Sam tried to pet him and touch his face with her hand, he winced and made a mournful cry. Once again, Smokey was rushed to the vet. Smokey was running a temperature and his gingivae were severely red. His teeth had horizontal cavities along the gum line. Under anesthetic, seven teeth were dissected and extracted. A special food and antibiotics were prescribed, and Smokey was back in the saddle.

This big pawed, cocklebur matted, and amusing Amish Maine coon lives on to this day.

Terrorist

Ode to Terrorist

There once was a cat named Terrorist.
His skills at night were the rarest.
Through a skylight he slipped, down to the scene,
'Twas at night to visit a queen.

Was it ravish or maybe true love?
Left the same way through the window above.
When the kittens came, he couldn't be found,
For Toronto Terrorist had already skipped town.

Caught by the law, taken to the pound.
Was on death row, till a family was found.
Immigrated to Iowa in the back of a car.
This cat's legend soon traveled afar.

The new digs were on Delta, the west part of town.
His reputation and talents were quickly renowned.
Other cats ran when he stepped out the door,
Even dogs disappeared when he let out a roar.

Terrorist did not always follow the rules,
That is till the day he lost his family "jewels".
In retirement, he lived on Hickory with a harem of cats,
Watched birds by the pool and was said to grow fat.

174

Stella Sandahl was a professor of Hindi at the University of Toronto. She was Swedish, trained in Paris, spoke four languages, traveled extensively in India and Southeast Asia, and had a unique passion. She was the very definition of a crazy cat lady. In fact, she could have been a poster child for the cause. She seemed to need to rescue cats for purposeful living.

Stella had a menagerie of cats. They all lived in a two-story house in an eclectic grouping of nineteenth-century Victorian homes along a canal close to the university. She had observed this bedraggled, longhaired, orange-colored cat starting to develop the round abdomen of pregnancy. Each evening at twilight, Stella quietly placed a bowl of rice laced with cream on the back steps.

"Here kitty, kitty, kitty," Stella's Swedish accent echoed in its staccato rhythm.

Stella watched the feral kitty come each night for her neighborhood handout. The kitty would inch its way from under the rusting VW van parked in the alley. Upon reaching the steps, Stella would say in her soothing voice, "See it's alright. You are safe with me."

Sally, as Stella named her, would ravenously clean out the bowl, looking up occasionally to make sure her surroundings were protected. This ritual occurred nightly. When the evening came that Sally did not appear, Stella set off with her flashlight, hopeful to find the momma cat and her newborns.

"Here kitty, kitty, kitty. Here kitty, kitty, kitty," Stella begged while pointing her flashlight under foundations, backyard sheds, and each window well of the eight houses facing the alley. Her hunt was rewarded when she got to the Stewart family's basement window where she found the mother, Sally, nursing one orange tabby and three coal black kittens. For the next week, Stella delivered "meals on wheels" to the window setting. One night, upon reaching the birthing nest, she found it empty. The blue blanket that she had laid under the mother and kittens had hair and an impression where Sally had been nesting. Stella set off on yet another search with her posse of friends. After exploring every possible hiding place in a two-block area, no signs were found of the mother cat and her kittens.

A month later during spring finals week, Stella spotted two kittens playing under the peony bushes in the driveway. Since one was black, Stella hoped that Sally had survived and brought her kittens out to teach them to use their instincts to hunt for food. Stella's own cats greeted her, doing the serpentine back and forth brushing of the bodies between her legs. They meowed impatiently for their dinner. She rationed out the kibble into ten colored Fiesta-ware saucers and placed them on the floor mat. Stella sang, "What's new Pussycat?" as she giddily portioned out another special bowl, adding some salmon to the rice and cream, and slipped out the back door past her own cats.

"Here kitty, kitty, kitty," she sang out. And there she was. Sally, now much thinner despite her pendulous mammary glands, came running. Four kittens peeked out from the flowerbed. "You dear old momma, where have you been hiding? And you brought all of the kittens to see me too!"

The largest, the orange and white kitten, was the most aggressive, and hissed and lifted his hackles when touched.

Stella's kitchen was open to Sally and her wild brood for several more weeks. One by one, she was able to catch three of the kittens and took them to the vet's office to have them spayed. The biggest kitten refused to be caught or tamed. It became visibly apparent that this was a young tomcat.

The seasons passed and the new school year, with the Toronto winter, was giving way to the blooming of spring. The warmer weather allowed Stella to leave her windows in the dormer open for the fresh fragrances of March to filter into the upstairs. A skylight on the roof was left open at night for ventilation for the stuffy office.

Stella had retired for the evening and had turned off the lights in her bedroom when she was startled by the shrieking meow and guttural growling sounds of a cat fight in the house. Putting on her slippers, she rushed to the study and flipped on the light. She was just in time to see an orange, blurry image spring from the floor to the desk and leap to the lip of the skylight. It hung there by its front claws momentarily as Stella reached for a broom. Swinging precariously, this midnight demon finally scratched with both rear feet and escaped to the roof. "You dirty terrorist," Stella hollered. She noticed her latest rescue cat, Martha, was watching the whole spectacle from the overstuffed leather chair.

It did not take a college professor to figure out that the sex drive of the young alley cat had helped it find this remote way into the house to come calling on Martha. Stella knew immediately that this orange and white midnight visitor must be the untamed kitten from Sally's litter of last year. She had dubbed him the Terrorist, and now it was her turn to surprise him.

Stella went to a shelf in her garage and pulled down her live trap and dusted off the cobwebs. She laced and baited it with salmon and milk, and Terrorist was caught the next night as he came prowling for a repeat performance. His hissing, pawing, and frustration at being restrained gave Stella satisfaction as she loaded the wobbly cage in her Subaru Outback and sped off to the vet's office.

"It's your unlucky day—you little Terrorist! Last night was your final time to spread your genes in the Cat Kingdom," Stella chatted to the movement in the back of the SUV.

And so it was, this Toronto Terrorist became an "It." Over time, Terrorist's manners seemed to mellow, and he even allowed Stella to pet and coo over him. Calling "Kitty, kitty, kitty" immediately brought this orange racer from several houses away, or down from a tree where he had been perched.

What ultimately happened to Terrorist requires a pause to introduce a young couple who lived in an upstairs apartment across the alley. They had just had a baby.

* * * *

Lou Fenech was a graduate student at the university on a postdoctoral fellowship in Asian studies. His sweet wife, Christine, was from England and a feline aficionado. This new mother was stunningly beautiful and with a charming wit. Christine had been raised along the English Channel in Brighton and Cornwall. Lou was a Canadian, and they met two continents away while backpacking and exploring the northern Thailand countryside. Christine had been traveling with her friend, Caroline, who was blind, and together they were navigating and exploring the world. They bumped into Lou Fenech as they were stopped at the Laotian border. Lou, several years younger, was debonair with gorgeous, brown, penetrating eyes and olive skin. He had a handsome face and bubbling personality. They were halted and turned away from crossing the bridge as a civil war in Laos prohibited travel. As brave kids in their twenties, they had a different thought about the warning and precautions. They only wanted to see the other side of the mountain and the lush, forested Laotian countryside. No dice!

After being turned away, the three went their separate directions. Several months later, Christine and Caroline accidently crossed paths in southern Thailand and backpacked off to Bangkok where they bumped into Lou at a food market and instantly reunited with nonstop talking and sharing their last two months' experiences. This serendipitous reunion stoked a love affair between Christine and Lou, which had roots from previous meetings in Canada and Gstaad, Switzerland. Meanwhile, Christine and Caroline extended their wayward journey for the next seventeen months in Australia and New Zealand. Letters and phone calls brought Christine and Lou to New York City for Christmas in 1987. They soon married and returned to Toronto for Lou to finish his post-doctoral work.

Stella had befriended the young couple as Lou was in her department at the university. They had already adopted one of the kittens from Terrorist's midnight caper. Now Stella suggested the Feneches might be interested in another cat. "He is a perfectly tame guy now and just needs some domesticating." Lou had just taken a teaching job in the states, and the Feneches agreed there was no way they could fly to Iowa with a baby and their own cats.

Stella thought for a moment and said, "Here's an offer. How about I drive you there, and we will take your baby and the cats, including the one I call Terrorist?"

"Christine, it's your call," Lou said.

"If you don't mind, my dear, the Terrorist may come with us," Christine said with a giddy smile.

The plot was set, though none of them had ever been to the Midwest, much less Iowa. Lou had flown out to the small airport at Waterloo in the late winter for an interview. The History Department at the University of Northern Iowa had offered him a teaching position. His intellect, research, and knowledge of the Far East, India, and Asia was his ticket to the position.

The 811-mile trip in August to Iowa in a Subaru Outback without air conditioning was in motion. Stella with her husband Tim, Lou and Christine with their seven-month-old baby boy Hano, and three cats—Vivicka, Digga, and Terrorist—were all squeezed into the hatchback. They towed a U-Haul trailer.

Terrorist had only been in a car for trips to the vet clinic, so he meowed incessantly in the pet taxi, trying desperately to open the cage door with both front paws. The adults conferred and opted to see how he would behave outside the pet carrier. After leaving the Toronto traffic, the cage door was unlatched. It was like opening a whole new world for Terrorist. He calmly jumped to the front seat and perched himself next to the headrest. He watched intently for the rest of the journey like a sea captain navigating the high seas. Every approaching car, sign, truck, overpass, tree, and city landscape met his eyes. The stern look on his face suggested study of every oncoming object like a detective looking for a clue. At rest stops, all three cats were put on leashes and allowed out of the car to stretch and use the litter pan if they chose. Neither of the other two cats seemed to interest Terrorist as he hurried back to the car, jumped in the side door, and scurried back to the navigator seat next to the driver. Terrorist had taken to this cross-country trip like a backpacker on a mission.

Nearing the Indiana border, the adrenaline of this crew started to wane. Sandwiches and bottled water had kept them going for the first four-hundred miles. It was decided to pull over for the night at a motel at exit twenty-two. The noise from the interstate hummed all night. Four adults, a baby, and three cats all attempted to settle in for the night. Terrorist sat up all night on his haunches with a switching of his tail the only movement as he stared at the blinds drawn over the window.

After a short night, the traveling troop ate a hasty breakfast at the nearby Perkins Restaurant and filled their water bottles. Terrorist was already sitting patiently in the car on guard duty looking out the front window. He seemed to know by all the loading of the car that there was more travel ahead. He panted to cool himself, waiting for the car to move. It was "Iowa or Bust" with the vents open, windows down, and full speed ahead.

Arriving at Cedar Falls in the late afternoon, they were greeted at the rental house on Delta Drive. The head of the department, Rich Newell, and his wife Nancy had arranged this temporary home for the new faculty member and his family. To everyone's surprise, Stella screamed, "Is that you Nancy? Oh my God! The last time I saw you we were in Delhi sharing a beer together!" The reunion continued as the Feneches looked on in wonderment of the moment with the outpouring of kindness to their family.

Rich asked, "Do you have a car? You will need one to get around as this is far from the campus and any grocery store. I have a second car that I will be happy to loan you until you can get on your feet and get your own wheels." Inside the house, the new family was astonished to find the refrigerator filled with food. Was this "Iowa nice" or what!

Terrorist scoped out the house and peered out the sliding glass door at a cornfield in the backyard. The big city alley cat and world traveler now had a farm in the backyard. Sitting on his haunches, he saw birds and grasshoppers flipping freely across the yard. He nattered with anticipation at the hunting paradise within his reach. Christine, watching him look out toward the sinking sun in the west, spoke in her sweetest British accent, "You dear kitty, can you believe our fortunes? Our life has been so blessed, you little demon. I'll get you outside soon."

Terrorist thought, *She has no idea. When this door is open, this new yard will be my hunting mecca.*

After the boxes were unpacked and the beds made, Terrorist was allowed out the back door. He crouched and crept on his belly in his newfound wilderness. No rabbit, bird, or insect was safe. Dogs on leashes cowered as he stalked and intimidated them with his guttural growl and showing of his teeth.

The Feneches soon purchased their first home on Hickory Lane in an established neighborhood of 1930s-built homes. The homes were closer together and the yards much smaller. A fence was soon built around the yard with a forty-five-degree angle, inward bevel at the top which would have kept even the great Houdini from climbing to escape. Terrorist now had his own yard and a cat door to the kitchen. He shared it with Vivicka, Digga, and a recently-adopted cat, Floosy.

Floosy had been hit by a car on Rainbow Drive when Christine happened upon the scene. Laying there in shock, the cat was quickly grabbed and rushed to the vet, who examined her and pronounced her to be unharmed except for some road rash.

The yard became a no-fly-zone for any bird that dared to do aerial reconnaissance. All insects were fair game. Chipmunks played "cat and munk" with Terrorist always the victor. He proudly brought the carcasses into the house and dropped them on the bed to show his prowess and to receive praise. The bat dropped on the dining room table did not receive the high praise he anticipated, nor did the baby bunnies he saved under the beds so that he could enjoy them later. He was the King of the Roost, and Christine called him "one hasty creature" when it came to his ability to appreciate other fauna in their quaint British-style courtyard.

Eventually, Terrorist started the nasty habit of peeing down a heat vent in the kitchen. One can only imagine the stench of heated cat urine permeating through the house in the winter. Several attempts to discipline him proved fruitless, including hair spray on the vents, spraying him with vinegar when he neared a vent, and placing sticky tape on the floor around the vents. The final remedy was to remove all the floor vents and have the heating ducts raised higher on the wall.

In time, Christine was to rival her Canadian friend, Stella, for the title of poster-child for crazy cat ladies. Leona, a longhaired tortie who was a true street walker, came to live with the family. She loved the outside and would not come in the cat door all summer, preferring the fenced courtyard. Demetri, a black and white male, seemed to say, *Okay ladies, I'll put up with letting Terrorist rule this kingdom.*

Hano was eventually joined by a sister, Agatha. They became musicians and thespians at school. Their love for all their great cat friends was immense. While the siblings were in high school, Terrorist became extremely ill. Christmas Day found the whole family at my office. Terrorist was advanced in age. He was dehydrated, and diagnosed with kidney failure. He was given a good dose of fluids intravenously while the family sat in the waiting room. There was no Christmas dinner at the Feneche's that year. They had spent all morning at the vet's worrying and waiting for Terrorist to be released. Terrorist's return home that afternoon was one special Christmas gift for the family.

Christine learned to give Terrorist subcutaneous fluids with two large sixty milliliter syringes each day to keep him hydrated. He managed to crawl out the cat door and sit in the warm winter sunlight every day.

At the age of eighteen, this proud street fighter died in Christine's arms. "Oh, my dear Rum Tum Tugger. My bad boy. You were such a rebel, but my Rock Star." While she sat up late that night in her rocking chair, she sang *Memories* from Andrew Lloyd Webber's *Cats*. She had seen it as a teenager at the New London Theatre.

Tigger

BOINK

BOINK

Ode to Tigger

There once was a cat named Tigger.
'Twas scrawny but grew much bigger.
Bouncy! Bouncy! Much like Pooh's friend.
Slowed by age, 'couch potato' at end.

A pound a year, not an ounce more.
This dude lived to twenty-four.
Svelte athlete and bouncy by name.
With his girth, a Rum Tum Tigger became.

With all his claws, he was well armed.
From earthworms to spiders, nothing he harmed.
A picture of health, but to his chagrin,
Blackheads and zits appeared on his chin.

This hunter and lover had many lives.
Stayed clear of the log filled with beehives.
Prowled round the house when others in bed.
Watching the moon and dreaming instead.

Helped in the garden in his heyday.
From concord grapes, kept the pigeons away.
This intelligent cat, TV news was his 'biz,
Cronkite his favorite, 'and that's the way it is'!

"Mommy! Mommy! Mommy!" came the excited scream from five-year-old Maria Christina. "You won't believe what followed me home from school." Cuddled in her arms was a small black and white kitten which she hoped would be able to live in the family's "dogs only" household. Hans and Renata knew their daughter had a deep passion and love for animals and the outdoors. Her excitement tugged at their hearts.

A trip to Dr. Kleaveland's veterinary office confirmed that this kitten, named Pricilla, was a boy, but the name stuck. The vet performed the standard healthcare routine for kittens—treating runny eyes and conjunctivitis. Pricilla vomited a worm that morning, confirming that he had vermin. Following a dose of wormer, the evacuation of the wiggly, glistening worms turned Maria's mother's stomach.

Pricilla ruled the household in no time. The family's dog, Gunther, quickly learned that this foreign agent had daggers at the end of its feet. Pricilla employed his Halloween cat stance with raised hackles, arched back, and a steady hiss warning, *Back off big boy, unless you want your eyes clawed out*. Pricilla had a penchant for being outdoors. He never ventured far from the house in the family's huge, wooded lot. Hiding behind the neatly corded wood pile, he watched nature's smallest creatures in action. Spiders, snails, crickets, and his favorite—fireflies—performed for him.

When he was three years old, the first cold snap of November brought a dusting of snow to the woods. A car parked in the driveway had something dripping underneath which drew his attention. Pricilla explored the puddle. He found the liquid had a sweet taste and it melted the snow as it trickled down the sloping driveway. Within hours of coming back inside from the cold outdoors, Pricilla started vomiting and staggering like a drunk. This twelve-pound, healthy cat had never been sick a day in his life. The retching continued about every fifteen minutes through the night. The next morning, he was rushed to see Dr. Kleaveland. A kidney function test confirmed the doctor's first premonition that Pricilla's days were numbered. The antifreeze from the visiting clunker car parked in the family's driveway was the culprit. Antifreeze ingestion is irreversible. It fries the kidneys and crystallizes the descending nephrons. Pricilla was laid to rest.

Maria was heartbroken and sadly learned the hazards of chemicals and accidental exposure and contact with them. When her tears subsided, she secured the promise from her mommy and dad that another kitty would be found for her, but acquisition of her new kitten needed to be postponed as Aunt Julianna was coming to visit from Germany for three weeks. Mother Renata declined to have a new kitten and a house busy with her excitable sister-in-law at the same time.

The Sunday trip to the Waterloo airport arrived, and there was lots of hugging and waving goodbye to the departing auntie under the airport canopy. As the family's Lincoln motor started to take them home again, so did the demand from Maria in the backseat, "And now we can go get the kitten!"

"What do you mean now? And what kitten are you talking about?" came the astonished reply from her mother.

"Oh, it's just on the way home over at Jenny Nadler's house on Winter Ridge. It's not far from here," Maria explained with the direct manner of a nine-year-old.

Little girls have a way of turning their father's hearts into mush. Big daddy Hans acquiesced and drove the family to the Nadler's home in the woods. The Nadlers seemed to be expecting them. As the Lincoln coasted down the hilly, winding road, the whole family was gathered in the front yard to greet them. Jenny had boxed up the mother cat and four kittens to help sell the inevitable new kitten for Maria. Her selection was orange colored and, again, with rather runny eyes and a pot belly. It was Tigger's lucky day.

Why do so many kittens have runny eyes, often accompanied with an abundance of intestinal parasites from roundworms to coccidia (tiny parasites living in the intestinal walls)?

Sure enough, as the family's veterinarian, I confirmed the next day that this was more than just a skin-and-bones, sneezing kitten. Tigger had a respiratory infection, as well as a high fever. I was reluctant to treat the kitten with such a fever and a distended belly full of worms. I prescribed some antibiotics drops for twenty-four hours to fight the lung infection first.

That night, Maria's mother religiously administered the pink liquid drops with an eye dropper. By morning, it was apparent that the fever had broken. Tigger was returned to the vet for deworming and a bath. Out came the worms and in went the new food. Within a few days, Tigger became a bouncy-bouncy kitten, much like his namesake from *Winnie the Pooh*, happily settled in at Maria's home to reign supreme.

* * * *

"Mommy. Mommy. Mommy!" Maria was screaming at the top of her lungs. "Tigger's got a mouse or something in his mouth," she cried. Tigger had been prowling around the woodpile in the backyard. He was carrying something into the house. With his head held high, strutting with pride, he stopped at the doorstep and dropped the treasure.

"Oh my God!" Renata shouted. "This is no mouse. I think it is a baby kitten!"

Maria begged, "Well, we have to help it!" Tigger stood by with his head turned halfcocked, seeming to enjoy the mayhem he had created. A baby kitten that does not have its eyes opened presents a challenge even for the best of nursemaids. Baby formula, baby nursing bottles, hot water bags . . . Maria had the determination to save the kitten's life, and it paid dividends. By the time the kitten's eyes opened, it had acquired the name of Samantha. In due time, just as her rescuer had experienced, Samantha was taken to the vet for its kittenhood vaccinations and health examination. Upon lifting the tail, the vet confirmed that Samantha was Sam. The name was not changed to protect Samantha's identity.

Samantha was brought home and, for the first time following the clean health exam, allowed to come in off the porch and in contact with Tigger, who had been "king of the jungle" for three years. It was not a slam dunk. How should he treat this interloper? After all, he was the one who had rescued the mouse-like creature. They smelled each other, and each made a half-hearted hiss. Tiny Samantha ran under Tigger's long legs and batted at his bushy tail. They flopped down on the Turkish area rug and rolled over, holding each other in their paws. It was the beginning of a friendship that lasted for more than twenty years.

Two leather butterfly high-back chairs in the den became the cats' thrones. They took daily naps with Tigger holding Samantha in his arms like a baby. They purred with contentment as they slumbered—each with a dreamy facial expression and eyes closed.

* * **

Tigger was the hunter for the family. Squirrels taunted him while he stood guard in the vineyard. The black walnut trees were their hangouts and became the battleground. While Tigger made his morning rounds, the bushy-tailed red squirrels chattered insults. Tigger sat at attention, staring at the prey until they finally retreated to the neighbor's pine trees.

Pigeons seemed to be addicted to the concord grapes in the family's vineyard. They often met their Waterloo when, with Elmer Fudd-like tenacity, Hans took aim with his Daisy BB gun. His greatest fear was the great orange cat, Tigger, who had the ability to disappear among the vines and leap vertically to nab these flighty grape thieves in midair. Hans did not want to hit the cat with the BB gun.

Tigger had a great sense of humor. The peony bushes in full bloom were his cover for attack. He must have had a timepiece, because he laid in waiting for the mistress of the house to come home from work. As the car drove up the drive it was all eyes forward and his whiskers started to twitch. The victim would open the car door and approach. On the count of three, the attack commenced. Without hesitation, Tigger leaped at Renata's legs and wrapped himself around them, affectionately welcoming her home. This surprise attack was always rewarded by a scream and shriek and, "You crazy cat—it's so nice to see you—let's go inside and have some tea."

❉❉

The friendship of Tigger and Samantha was steadfast. They lolled away the days sleeping in the warm sunlight at the east bay window. They watched Maria go to school along the sidewalk with her pigtails bouncing. When she became a busy teenager, it was the love of her father, Hans, the cats sought. Tigger's long hair would form dreadlocks if it was not combed out daily. The routine became waiting for the pickup door to close, then hopping down and running to the back door to wait for Hans. His deep bass voice sent out a greeting, and the cats and their master jabbered in cat-talk, telling one another about their day. The cats jumped into his lap as they watched the evening news together. They stared at the flashing TV screen, seeming intent on understanding the world's events each day.

When Maria left home for college, Tigger was most distressed. He examined her bedroom and his longing, lonesome meow-meow followed as he slowly walked around the house looking for her. Up the stairs, onto Maria's bed, into the den, around the kitchen, he looked and waited for her return.

At last, at quarter break, Maria did return home. She hugged and cuddled her cat. They retreated to her bedroom. Tigger listened with his head tilted as he attempted to understand about school, parties, and dorm life. He sat and listened but seemed to sense that things were only temporary. Looking at the suitcase lying open on the floor, he knew that she would soon be leaving again.

Tigger became Hans's cat. Walter Cronkite's voice brought the big cat from his resting perch in the butterfly chair to hop onto Hans's lap to catch the latest in the world. When Tigger heard, "And that's the way it was on this day, October . . ." he knew dinner was soon to follow.

Tigger was all about fish. The can opener's vibration mesmerized him and the intoxicating smell of any kind of fish made him salivate. He tolerated the kibble dry food, but it was no replacement for fish.

Tigger grew into a couch potato while he whiled away the day sleeping and lying in the sun. Resting and spending the winter trapped inside were not kind to his waistline. He put on weight at about a pound a year, which followed him into his twenties, though he was seldom sick with only an occasional hairball disrupting his love of food.

Hans found Tigger at the age of twenty-four staggering around the house with a starry, glazed look in his eyes. He had been losing weight and was not able to jump up into the butterfly chairs anymore. "Old friend, I knew this day had to come. We have talked about life together and have been each other's listening posts. You have been the most special guy I have ever known. I promised that whichever one of us went first, there would be no pain. I think it's your time," Hans memorialized his big orange friend and massaged him under his chin which always was Tigger's favorite place to be touched. The purring started one last time.

As the car started to back down the driveway, big tears formed and rolled down Hans's cheeks. He carried Tigger into my office and we both knew it was Tigger's time to go. We embraced and blubbered our words of both sadness and great friendship we shared over this great, bouncy, long-haired orange cat named Tigger.

Tony T

Ode to Tony T

Hey diddle diddle, this cat loved to fiddle.
But no cow or spoons for this little riddle.
This cat lived deep in the heart of Texas.
His dancing owner drove a hot Lexus.

Came from a friend, for a short time to take.
Named after Tony the Tiger, but he was no flake.
Loved everything country, *Boot Scootin' Boogie* his song.
He walked with a swagger, and his legs were long.

His lady away, consulted out of town.
Tony cleared the mantel, keepsakes to the ground.
Cat sitters came twice daily to check on him.
But revenge piddling on new boots, no hearts did win.

Tony and the lady moved often, like gypsies.
She loved dancing and dressed really glitzy.
Met a handsome man who came to live.
Tony ruled the house, not an inch did give.

Respiratory problems with congestive heart signs.
Had his chest drained multiple times.
Slowed with coughing, his time had come.
This confident Texan's days were done.

This lanky Texan sauntered onto the Deer Park School administrative grounds. The stranger's riveting green eyes suggested mystery in his past. A perfect, unique, dark black "M" across his forehead accented this gray and black tabby's face. Like the "Z" of Zorro or Harry Potter's lightning bolt, it was a distinctive accent for his personality. He had alternating tan and black ring patterns in his hair, extending all the way to the tip of his tail. Like a sail mast, it stood at attention as he paraded the grounds. With an air of confidence and persona of being in control, this cat met Tricia, the big-hearted director of special education, as she crossed the parking lot on a Friday afternoon in late-fall.

"Here kitty, kitty," Tricia beckoned to this beautiful cat. With confidence and a John Wayne-like swagger, the cat came straight into her arms.

"I just can't leave you here. Where do you live? You look so thin. You must be hungry. I was fixin' to go dancing tonight with a friend. What am I supposed to do with you? Well, come with me and we'll see what I can come up with as a shelter," the pretty lady chatted with the cat.

The big tabby massaged his whiskered face, first on one side and then the other, of Tricia's smooth, powdered face. She hugged him and kissed his forehead, then unlocked her black BMW. The steamy hot car was soon blasting cool air into their faces. They sped onto the on-ramp of the freeway and headed for Tricia's place. It was an unconventional home, as the lady lived on a sailboat in Galveston Harbor. This saga cannot be made up!

This stray was introduced to the two dogs, Sami and Tuli, and a cat, Miss Piggy, already living aboard the sailboat. The big Texan tabby walked onto the boat deck and surveyed the galley like he was casing the joint. Tricia had some canned tuna and extra clay litter in a sealed container from a previous cat-rescue mission. She frantically scurried about gathering supplies—a used Sara Lee pie tin, a few toys, and a small cat bed she had stowed under a deck bench. She was already running late to get on the road to pick up her dear friend, Cathy, who was also a special education consultant.

Tricia and Cathy were both single and often spent their weekend nights together at country bars. Western swing dancing in their tight-fittin' jeans, sequined designer blouses, and, of course, stylized cowboy boots made these career professionals look like they had just arrived from a day of pushing cattle. They joyfully forgot their days leading organizations in air-conditioned board rooms.

Tricia sped to arrive at Cathy's garden home in Pasadena about forty miles away. Cathy had been pacing, impatiently worried about her friend Tricia—Trichy as she affectionately drawled with her thick Texas accent. Tricia was punctual as clockwork, never late. Cathy was looking out the front bay window as the BMW whipped into the driveway. She was relieved that her friend was okay, but wondered what Tricia was carrying up the steps as she approached the door. Opening the door to greet her friend, Cathy was shocked to find a huge cat. He walked right in her door and into her life.

"Oh my god, Trichy, what do you have here?" Cathy gasped. They watched the cat as it strolled through the foyer without hesitation. The cat immediately walked away with his tail held high, exploring the rest of the condo.

"Trichy! He's gorgeous! But, but, but . . . what's he doing here?"

"Honest, Cath. The reason I am late is because he was in the parking lot this afternoon as I was leaving work. He looked so hungry and lost that I couldn't leave him there. I was hoping that you could keep him for a few days while I try to find where he lives or another home for him." Tricia was talking so fast that there was not even a chance for Cathy to turn down the request.

The cat was not in the least frightened, even though he had been dropped off so quickly at this "temporary" living spot. Tricia emptied a small cup of gray clay litter into the pie tin. Cathy could hardly believe that a cat would use such a small aluminum pie tin for a potty. Tricia assured her this was all her brother-in-law, the vet, ever used for litter at the vet clinic. Sure enough, as soon as the pan with a skimpy amount of litter was put down on the kitchen floor, it was baptized.

Cathy named him Tony T after the Kellogg's cereal cat because he exuded the same bravado as big Tony the Tiger on the TV commercial. He seemed to talk, and though he didn't stand on his back feet saying, "Grrrreat!" he was a spitting image of Tony the Tiger, too. With no other animals to keep Tony T company, Cathy filled the CD table with music by George Straight, Patsy Cline, Garth Brooks, Kenny Rogers, and Ann Murray. She pushed the power button, and the two ladies were off, giving Tony T free range of the house.

194

It was nearly midnight before the BMW lights flashed across the front window, and the two tired cowgirls arrived home. Any angst about what Tony T may have done in their absence was quickly relieved. Cracking open the front door, they found him sitting on a bar stool. The Debby Boone song "You Light up my Life" was prophetically resonating from the speakers.

Cathy and Tricia enjoyed hooting and scooting—western dancing and swinging to the sounds of Brooks and Dunn's "Boot Scootin' Boogie" at Gilley's and all the country bar scenes of south Texas. Mix in an occasional longneck Lone Star and a few cowboys, and these ladies would dance the night away. Honky-tonks were everywhere, from Club Bojangles, Shagnasty's, Big Texas Spring Dance Hall & Saloon, to Claudio's Restaurant & Piano Bar. The mechanical bull, the cracking sound from pool table balls, and the disc-sanded shuffleboard drew cowboys to compete with the locals. But it was dancing to live music that brought a crowd to do the western swing. Cathy had been a dancer since the age of three, and she spun around the waxed floor stage in her flashy boots with the best of the dancers. Whether there were cowboys present or not, she and Tricia were renowned at all of these bars for their rhythm and style.

** **

During a routine Saturday house cleaning, Cathy screamed as a snake slithered out of the dirt from a potted plant she had brought into the house the night before. Tony T was always such a helper with the dust mop, thinking it was a game to pounce as it slid across the floor. Where was he today when she needed him? The snake slid under the door into a closet. Cathy retreated, slammed the door, and squeezed a bath towel under it. Tony T sensed this was not a normal scream, and the slamming door and towel drew his vigilance. He sat on his haunches, tilting his head from side to side, seeming to pick up the faintest vibration from some varmint behind the towel-secured door.

Cathy was not a herpetologist by any means, but after about a month she hoped that the snake had died in the room with no food or water. She braved it and unblocked the door. She wanted to rescue the house plant that had not been watered in the interim. The surface of the potted plant had dried out, and with a spoon she slightly loosened the crust. She jumped back as she saw a feathery, dried snakeskin. She jumped again when the live snake frantically tried to slither over the pot edge. Often, it is best not to rehearse the "flight and fright" reaction. Without any hesitation, she grabbed the end of the tail as the snake once again was trying to serpentine across the carpeted floor. Holding her breath and tiptoeing through the kitchen, she opened the sliding glass door and tossed the uninvited guest out into the flower bed. Trying to regain her composure, she realized she was not alone in this adventure. There was Tony T, sitting high on a bar stool. He seemed to say, *You go girl. I am so happy you didn't need my help.*

There was always music and singing in the house, and those weekend nights with the music seemed to make a director out of Tony T. It was the fiddle music that he appeared to particularly like. It created a slight wiggle in his body as he sat perched on any elevated stool. At times, he was chosen to be Cathy's dance partner when a slow song played on the CD. Like the junior high dance drills, Cathy pulled Tony T onto the dance floor. He snuggled in Cathy's neck and they did the prettiest two-step. This was about the only time in his life that he ever let Cathy lead.

Tony T was very stand-offish toward strangers. He was even known to bite or scratch if they tried to pet or pick him up. Cathy loved to entertain her coworkers at her home. There was Nurse's Day, Speech Pathologist's Day, Music Appreciation Day, and Secretary's Day, just to name a few. At first for these gatherings, she tried to shut Tony T in the spare bedroom. He was always able to wrangle his way out and come sit on his favorite bar stool at the table like he was the co-host.

Cathy retired from her special education career and became a consultant, frequently traveling out of town overnight. A hired cat sitter came twice daily to entertain and recycle the CD music for Tony T. The cat did not like this separation, and at least twice got even with his cowgirl lady friend. Cathy had a beautiful pair of new designer boots still in the box in her closet. Tony T took it upon himself to open the boot box and piddle on the never-worn, tanned deerskin leather boots. When she returned home, Cathy noticed a reeking smell coming from the closet. The brand-new boots were ruined and had to be discarded. After another time of being left with a cat sitter and feeling lonely, Tony T climbed onto the fireplace mantel. He managed to wipe it clean of valuable keepsakes. As each crystal ornament crashed onto the tile floor below, he surely watched with amusement. When Cathy returned home, Tony T was sitting on the chaise lounge looking like the Cheshire Cat. He seemed to be saying, *That will teach you to leave me alone.*

Cathy met Jerry through dancing, and he became a frequent visitor. Tony T frowned. *Hey dude, she is my lady and dance partner. Keep your hands off!* When Jerry came to live with Cathy, Tony T shunned him for weeks. The cat growled if this new man tried to slip into Tony T's queen-sized bed. Sent to the couch, Jerry had to win over this four-legged, Texan.

After experiencing a severe coughing fit, Tony T was rushed to an emergency vet clinic. Was it allergies or something more critical? When the vet listened to Tony T's heart and lungs, they were very raspy and made a watery noise like there was fluid in his chest. She administered an antihistamine and a steroid for some immediate but temporary relief. Tony T came home, but there was definitely something more involved than allergies. Cathy scheduled an appointment for Tony T to be examined further with Dr. Brayley, a veterinary cardiologist. He performed an EKG and x-rays and diagnosed congestive heart failure. Over the course of the next month, Tony T had the fluid drained from his chest three times. With each draining, the intervening times between episodes became shorter. Spending his last night in the middle of the bed, Tony T gasped for breath. The gurgling and rattling sound echoed as his chest rose and fell. The next morning Cathy cradled her big Texas guy and headed to the vet, Tony T's final ride. The stereo in her car just happened to be turned to Garth Brooks. He was singing, "To Make You Feel My Love." Tears rolled down onto Cathy's pink suit jacket.

Somewhere deep in the heart of Texas, this confident cat with a western swagger is buried under a magnolia tree. This "night or two until I can find him a home" turned into thirteen wonderful years for Tony T and Cathy.

197

Acknowledgements

Without the help of the following to help tell their stories the family cat or edit the descriptions from the interviews, this story of Cats would not have been possible. I thank them again and trust that their memories and love of these cats with be now preserved in book form.

Holly Crandall
Ron Dornath
Christine Fenesch
Doris Gillespie
Tricia Groda
Marla Hool
Janie Hull
Shirley Johnson
Barbara Kenyon
Ann McGillicuddy
Megan McGillicuddy
Renata Sack
Cathy Sartain
Carolyn Kenyon Stafford
Tom Tritle and Kathy Kerr
Renee Veenstra
Samantha Zuback

About the Author

Dr. James Kenyon has been married for fifty years to Cynthia, the city girl who fell in love with a farm boy. They have three children: Jennifer is a school counselor married to Brook, a district judge; Carolyn is a veterinarian married to Christopher, an architect realtor; John is a graphic designer married to Kelsey, a marketing director. The Kenyons have six grandchildren.

James is a graduate of the Kansas State University College of Veterinary Medicine and a Kansas State Veterinary Distinguished Alumni recipient. He served in the US Army Veterinary Corps and was a major for thirteen years in the Army Reserves. James is an eight-time veterinary volunteer for the Iditarod Alaskan dog sled race. He is a past president of the Iowa Veterinary Medical Association as well as chairman of the Iowa Veterinary Medical Examining Board.

About the Illustrator

Thomas Marple grew up in Minnesota, splitting time between the north woods and a dairy farm. Tom's earliest memories are of drawing the rich life around him with his mother's encouragement. He has worked as a wrangler, cowboy, conservationist, printer, graphic designer, and professor at a local community college. Throughout it all he has managed to illustrate and journal. He, too, has volunteered for the Iditarod (where he met Jim Kenyon). His older brother completed the race in 1976. He has been married to Michele, the love of his life, for thirty-five years and lives in North Dakota.

Note from the Publisher

As the baby in a farm family, separated from my nearest sibling by nearly a decade, cats were my first dedicated companions. I spent many a childhood hour searching every outbuilding on the farm for the litters of kittens that I knew the wild barn mommas were hiding. It was my goal, each and every season, to find and tame as many of the wildlings as possible. Tiger, Mister, Peanut Butter, Sylvester, Tom, Mitsy, Peanut Butter 2, Groucho, Ginger, Zephy, Groucho Too, Woody Blue, and Galahad . . . these are just a few of the cats that took up space in my heart in the first seventeen years of my life.

My current feline friend, Dobby Grace, is a pint-sized cat with a giant-sized attitude. She is my lap kitty through countless book projects. She hates the grand-cats, full-sized siblings that we refer to as the "little cats," though they are now full grown. Benjamin Bean, a big gray and white polydactyl cat, features a shorter than normal tail with a crook in the end. His sister, Beatrice Bug, is black and white and classically cat-shaped with a sleek coat of hair. Portraits of the cats we miss—Schatzi, Maurice, and Sooterkin—hang on our wall among the family photos.

These cat stories span forty years of veterinary practice, and they highlight the heart of a man who clearly loves these animals. When James said, would you like to publish a book of cat stories, I thought, *why have I not published one before?* This is a book for every person who has ever loved a cat. These stories detail the joy of first meeting them, the heartbreak of having to say goodbye, and all the special moments in between.

My hope is that you have a purrrfectly wonderful time reading this book. It was a delight to publish.

Tracy Million Simmons
Publisher, Meadowlark Press

Books are a way to explore, connect, and discover. Reading gives us the gift of living lives and gaining experiences beyond our own. Publishing books is our way of saying—

We love these words,
we want to play a role in preserving them,
and we want to help share them with the world.